The War on Christmas

Battles in Faith, Tradition, and Religious Expression

Bodie Hodge

General Editor

First printing: October 2013

Master Books®, P.O. Box 726, Green Forest, AR 72638

Master Books® is a division of the New Leaf Publishing Group, Inc.

ISBN: 978-0-89051-790-1

Library of Congress Number: 2013948497

Cover Design: Left Coast Design

Interior Design: Diana Bogardus

Unless otherwise noted, Scripture quotations are from the New King James Version of the Bible.

Please consider requesting that a copy of this volume be purchased by your local library system.

Printed in the United States of America

Please visit our website for other great titles:
www.masterbooks.net

For information regarding author interviews,
please contact the publicity department at (870) 438-5288

Photo Credits: T-top, B-bottom, L-left, R-right, C-Center, BK-Background

Creation Museum: pg 110, pg 140, pg 142

Wikimedia Commons: pg 8, pg 33, pg 35, pg 92, pg 97, pg 101, pgs 102-103, pg 131 — Images from Wikimedia Commons are used under the CC-BY-SA-3.0 license or the GNU Free Documentation License, Version 1.3.

flickr: pg 53 Tom Taylor, Greenville S.C., pg 117 dianabog (Diana Bogardus)

istockphoto.com: pg 19, pg 39, pg 113, pg 114, pg 116, pg 120, pg 139 T

Dreamstime.com: pg 43, pg 91, pg 112

NASA: pg 81 T, pgs 82-83

Shutterstock.com: pg 7, pg 9, pg 11, pg 12, pg 15, pg 16, pg 17, pg 20, pg 21, pg 23, pg 25, pg 26, pg 27, pg 28, pg 29, pg 30, pg 31, pg 36, pg 38, pg 40, pg 44, pg 47, pg 50, pg 51, pg 52, pg 55, pg 56, pg 57, pg 58, pg 61, pg62, pg 63, pg 67, pg 68, pg 69 (2), pg 71, pg 72, pg 76, pg 81 B, pg 84, pgs 86-87, pg 89, pg 95, pg 98, pg 104, pg 105, pg 106, pg 108, pg 111, pg 121, pg 122, pg 123, pg 125, pg 126, pg 129, pg 133, pg 134, pg 135, pg 137, pg 139 B,

TABLE OF CONTENTS

Christmas. Who would attack Christmas? Hard to believe, isn't it? But Christmas is under attack. I would like to give some background as to why this beautiful holiday has caused such controversy.

Many years ago, much of the Western World was heavily Christianized and many people believed in God's Word as the authority. Then there was a subtle attack. It was so subtle that most Christians missed it. It was this idea that man could determine truth about origins apart from the Bible. When the Bible is left out, God is left out. So man, by default, becomes that authority. This is known as the religion of humanism, when man is elevated to a position of authority above God.

Since then, we have seen God and His Word attacked in every area as humanists demand the removal of God and His Word from every area of life. They do this to favor their own religion, which treats man as supreme above God. We have seen:

1. Christian-based public schools and universities (Harvard, Yale, Princeton, etc.) become humanistic;

2. The Bible removed from schools;

3. Prayer removed from schools;

4. Creation removed from schools;

5. The Pledge of Allegiance removed from use;

6. Attacks on the U.S. motto "In God We Trust";

7. Removal of 10 Commandments from public places;

8. Attempts to force acceptance of the sin of homosexual behavior upon Christian institutions and churches.

With these types of attacks, did we really believe that Christmas would be left alone? We now see conflicts surrounding Christmas in the form of refusals to say "Merry Christmas" but instead "Happy Holidays," the forced removal of Nativity scenes in public (and even some private) places, writing *X-mas* instead of *Christmas*, and even claims that Christmas was originally pagan!

Yes, there is a war on Christmas, and Christians need to know about this holiday and how to defend it, if they choose to celebrate it. This book is intended to provide some answers concerning a host of issues and misconceptions surrounding Christmas, and will look extensively at the very first Christmas. We want to proclaim the authority of the Bible from the very first verse of Scripture. God is the authority and this false religion of humanism needs to go.

If we as Christians do not know what we are celebrating, how can we share this good news of Christ with unbelievers? I pray this book is informative, equipping, and a blessing to you and your family all year long.

What

....

About

Happy Holidays!

Christmas?

CHAPTER 1

Christmas
and a
Humble Christ

Black Friday! What do you think of when you hear those words? Spectacular deals for Christmas? The (un)official beginning of the Christmas season? The worst day ever for anyone in retail or food service? Regardless of what pops into your head when you hear those words, the phrase bears a special meaning — at least in the Western World. It reminds us we need to start buying gifts for our family and friends.

The Christmas season is wrought with traveling, family get-togethers, office parties, breaks from school, and insane deals on flat-screen televisions. And let's not forget Santa Claus, hanging the stockings, decorating the tree, eating copious amounts of delicious food, and opening presents. Does this describe your Christmas?

Unfortunately, this probably describes the majority of people in America (and around the world). But what's the real reason for Christmas? Most people could probably answer this question by stating "the birth of Christ." But are we truly celebrating the birth of Christ? Sure, the wise men brought Him gifts, but they also worshipped Him. While we give gifts to each other, ask yourself what gift you are bringing to Him. The wise men knew the significance of Christ, so they brought Him gifts and worshipped Him.

But the true gift of Christmas is Christ — the Son of God, who became a man and willingly sacrificed Himself for the atonement of our sins to save us from a justly deserved eternal punishment. We are blessed exceedingly by this gift but only seem to celebrate it once a year, although we should be celebrating year-round. Do we truly understand who Jesus is and what He did? We'll be taking a closer look at this. In the meantime, forget about all the secular Christmas hype, focus on what you are giving to Christ, and worship Him.

And she brought forth her firstborn Son, and wrapped Him in swaddling cloths, and laid Him in a manger, because there was no room for them in the inn.

— Luke 2:7

Nativity scene on the 2001 Christkindlmarket in downtown Chicago. Christkindlmarket is a Christmas market held annually at Daley Plaza in Chicago, Illinois, United States. The festival is part of the Magnificent Mile Lights Festival and attracts more than 1 million visitors each year.

WHY DID CHRIST COME IN SUCH A HUMBLE AND LOWLY WAY?

After a supernatural conception, Christ was born through natural means. He was carried in the womb and was born as a helpless, vulnerable, powerless, and dependent newborn (of course, God supervised everything so He was never at risk). He didn't come to earth as a conquering angel or a mighty emperor. His parents were poor and probably had little livestock of their own (Luke 2:24; Leviticus 12:8), not to mention they were from Nazareth, an area not held in high regard, even Nathanael said, *"Can anything good come out of Nazareth?"* (John 1:46).

It's difficult to think of something more humble, vulnerable, and lowly than a newborn. God could have entered into this world as the Angel of the Lord, but He chose a much more humble way. Christ's incarnation was a reflection of God's character and heart. He was the utmost example to us of how to approach and present ourselves before the Father (Luke 18:17).

Proverbs 29:23 tells us that *"the humble in spirit will retain honor."* We know that Christ was the most humble of all who have lived on earth, even though He was and is also God, but for our sake He humbled Himself. And because of His humble state, He was given the highest honor:

. . . who, although He existed in the form of God, did not regard equality with God a thing to be grasped, but emptied Himself, taking the form of a bond-servant, and being made in the likeness of men. Being found in appearance as a man, He humbled Himself by becoming obedient to the point of death, even death on a cross. For this reason also, God highly exalted Him, and bestowed on Him the name which is above every name (Philippians 2:6–9; NASB).

According to Isaiah 57:15, God dwells *"with the contrite and lowly of spirit in order to revive the spirit of the lowly and to re-*

...I dwell in the high and holy place, With him who has a contrite and humble spirit, To revive the spirit of the humble, And to revive the heart of the contrite ones.
— *Isaiah 57:15*

vive the heart of the contrite" (NASB). God desires to lift us up from our lowly position, even if we suffer from a broken heart or a crushed spirit.

Christ's lowly condition should always remind us how we are supposed to approach the Father. God also uses the weak to shame the strong (1 Corinthians 1:26–29). God came in weakness so He could shame those who were looking for a strong political leader and were blind to their spiritual needs.

Such thoughts are but an introduction to what hope to have in this book. We hope to get into the meaning of Christmas, the origin of Christmas, misconceptions surrounding Christmas, and other aspects (including some of the debate surrounding Christmas) that you may not have heard of. Our hope is that you grow in your spiritual life by learning about this popular holiday with your Bible in hand as you examine the popular topics surrounding Christmas.

The Church of the Nativity, in Bethlehem. The door was reduced in size as a defense against hostile forces.

CHAPTER 2

Where
did the name
Christmas Come From?

Christmas is actually a combination of *Christ* and *mas*. Some Christians do not like the name because they equate the suffix *"mas"* with "Mass." However, this is not correct because "mas" actually means "celebration." Therefore, Christmas simply means a "Christ Celebration;" we celebrate the birth of our Lord and Savior.

CAN WE CELEBRATE IT?

Some don't even like the name "Christmas" — namely those who do not profess a belief in the biblical God. Some nonbelievers are "offended" by the "religious" name. This is probably because the mention of the name "Christ" brings about conviction. But it is a Christian holiday that even non-

Christians often celebrate, without warrant. They often want the holiday, but they don't want the reason for the holiday.

This is common with other Christian holidays and special days. For example, a weekend is a Christian thing. God created in six days (Genesis 1; Exodus 20:11) and rested on the seventh as a pattern for us. Hence, the seventh day or Sabbath day was to be a day of rest. When Christ resurrected on the first day of the week, the early church met on that day called the Lord's Day (e.g., John 20:1,

19; Acts 20:7; 1 Corinthians 16:2; Revelation 1:10). So the Christian concept of a weekend was born — having Saturdays and Sundays as special days. In an atheistic worldview, why have days off for rest and reflection of the Lord's Resurrection?

Also, some non-Christians do what they can around Christmas to demote Christmas by refusing to say the common greeting "Merry Christmas" or "Happy Christmas" and replace it with "Happy Holidays." Little do they realize that *holidays* means *holy days*. A day cannot be holy unless a Holy God exists and makes things holy. Perhaps when someone says "Happy Holidays," an interesting reply would be to ask: "To which holy days from God do you refer?"

WHEN DID CHRISTMAS BEGIN? This may be hard to believe, but when Christ was born, there was a celebration and God made sure of it. Is this wrong? Angels celebrated this event perhaps like no other in history (Hebrews 1:6; Luke 2:11–14). People also came to worship Christ and praise God for this event (Matthew 2:2; Luke 2:20).

So although there was celebration of Christ's birth when He became a man and stepped into history born of a virgin, it was likely some time later that Christians began re-celebrating His birth. Early church father Sextus Julius Africanus mentioned December 25 in *Chronographiai* in about A.D. 221. So Christians were surely celebrating this date by around this time.

According to famed chronologist Archbishop Ussher, Christ was born around 4 B.C. What day was Jesus born? We don't know, nor does Scripture reveal this date. So the date selected as Christmas (December 25 by the Gregorian calendar) was probably not the date Jesus was born (see chapter 5 for more). The issue, though, isn't about the actual date but about taking time to remember Christ's entrance into the world.

SHOULD WE CELEBRATE CHRISTMAS? Some people have even suggested to me that Christmas was evil and we should not partake in it. The Bible says: *The earth is the LORD'S, and all its fullness, The world and those who dwell therein.*

(Psalm 24:1; NIV). So, if we give thanks and honor God in what we do (Ephesians 5:15–21), then how can it be evil?

Some have suggested that the day Christmas is celebrated was born out of a Roman pagan holiday (but it wasn't; see chapter 4 for more details). Then I remind them that we should honor and celebrate God on every day of the year. Why should we, as Christians, refuse to celebrate God on this day? We can serve God on any day and at any time. In fact the Bible encourages this: *I will praise you, Lord my God, with all my heart; I will glorify your name forever more* (Psalm 86:12). "Forever

I will praise You, O Lord my God, with all my heart, And I will glorify Your name forevermore.

— Psalm 86:12

more" includes the day we celebrate Christmas.

Some have reminded me of the decorated trees in Jeremiah 10:1–6. Explain that it wasn't the tree that was sin but the hearts of those who used them to honor false gods. If they had done it to honor God then the outcome would have been different. If someone honors God with a decorated tree (as opposed to false gods) then how can it be sinful?

Some have said to me that Christ never told people to honor His birth with a holiday. I remind them that Christ never forbade it, either. There is no reason to forbid anyone from honoring God on this day by remembering Jesus' birth. For those honoring God in a special way this holiday season, please remember that:

- Christmas should be a time when we remember that Jesus came to earth to save us from Adam's sin, when we recall that God became lower than the angels to be born, live, suffer, and die for us.

- Christmas should be a time for us to remember that we as Christians have an obligation to leave the comforts of our everyday life to help those less fortunate, just as Jesus did for all of us.

It is a time for us to answer the questions that non-Christians are asking when they come to church this holiday season. It is a time for us to explain to people who don't know God the bad news in Genesis as well as the good news in the Gospels so that they, too, may enjoy the free gift of salvation in Jesus Christ. Also, God did not forbid the celebration of this event by the angels or by men, so it may not be wise to forbid others who want to worship Christ on this event.

Paul, in Colossians 2:16–17, says: *So let no one judge you in food or in drink, or regarding a festival or a new moon or sabbaths, which are a shadow of things to come, but the substance is of Christ.*

If one wishes to celebrate Christmas, arguably the most popular Christian festival in history, then no one should judge you for it. Sadly though, some do and without biblical warrant.

CHAPTER 3

What is Christmas About?

It is unfortunate that many have forgotten what Christmas is really about. We agree that many of the Christian holidays we celebrate seem to have their original intent muffled, even by many Christians. Unfortunately, the elements of this celebration have been watered down and, at times, forgotten. They have become secularized (e.g., Santa Claus, elves, etc.)

However, it is time Christians take back Christmas in the name of our Lord and Savior Jesus Christ, for everything belongs to the Lord (Psalm 24:1; 1 Corinthians 10:26).

It would be wrong to condemn someone for celebrating Christmas or Easter (Resurrection Sunday). The "substance," the reasons for these holidays,

should come from Christ because they belong to Christ. The reason we celebrate these holidays is to remember Christ. However, if someone is fully convinced in their mind that they should not celebrate these holidays, that is fine as well (Romans 14:5) and they should not be criticized either.

Why not take the distorted pagan elements of Christmas and change them to biblical elements to honor Christ? Many question the Christmas tree and say that it represents the Asherah poles mentioned in

the OT. However, these poles are where false gods were worshiped, in honor of their false gods. However, Christians do not worship the Christmas tree or false gods. Let's give Christian meanings to all of these elements especially since everything is the Lord's: *The earth is the LORD'S, and all its fullness, The world and those who dwell therein* (Psalm 24:1).

When we look at a Christmas tree let's remember that it was promised that salvation would spring up from the root of Jesse (Isaiah 11:10). The Christmas tree can be a symbol of Christ coming into the world and bringing of the kingdom of God (e.g., Revelation 1:6). The tree, often an evergreen tree, is used as the Christmas tree in many

15

homes . . . in the middle of winter and this represents life, of which Christ brought to a world that was dead to sin.

Since Christ is the head of the Church, let the ornaments, garlands, and lights represent His followers who cling to Him. Alone they are not much, but together with Christ they make something beautiful. Obviously, the star on top of the tree would represent the star of Bethlehem that guided the wise men to the King of kings (Matthew 2). Or if it's an angel, remember how Christ's birth was announced by a host of angels (Luke 2:8–14). Now, I'm saying don't do this if you don't want, but if you do, then use these as teaching points to the next generation.

What about giving gifts? One reason Christians give gifts is to remember the presents the wise men gave to Jesus, often times to those they love or to those in need. Consider also: *"for I was hungry and you gave Me food; I was thirsty and you gave Me drink; I was a stranger and you took Me in; I was naked and you clothed Me; I was sick and you visited Me; I was in prison and you came to Me.'*

Then the righteous will answer Him, saying, 'Lord, when did we see You hungry and feed You, or thirsty and give You drink? When did we see You a stranger and take You in, or naked and clothe You? Or when did we see You sick, or in prison, and come to You?' And the King will answer and say to them, 'Assuredly, I say to you, inasmuch as you did it to one of the least of these My brethren, you did it to Me (Matthew 25:35–40).

If we give to those in need, we are giving to the Lord (Proverbs 19:17). During the Christmas season (and throughout the rest of the year) let us remember those who are less fortunate and remember that in giving to them we are giving to the Lord. Here are some other passages to consider: Psalm 41:1; 112:5–9; Isaiah 58:10; Luke 14:13–14; Acts 20:35; Hebrews 13:16.

Perhaps you may have different ideas about how to celebrate Christmas, but my hope is that we can take back Christmas from the pagan elements that have infiltrated it, along with every other holiday (i.e., Holy Day).

...For I was hungry and you gave Me food; I was thirsty and you gave Me drink; I was a stranger and you took Me in; I was naked and you clothed Me; I was sick and you visited Me; I was in prison and you came to Me.

—Matthew 25:35–36

CHAPTER 4

The Origin of Christmas: Isn't

Christmas a Pagan Holiday?

This is a common but good question — especially around the Christmas season — and the answer is much deeper than most realize. Up front, the Bible simply doesn't give us the date of Christ's entrance into the world, so any estimates would only be inferences. But first, let's discuss this alleged "pagan" holiday.

There are various forms of paganism. Paganism began shortly after sin (Genesis 4:26; 1 John 3:12), likely with Cain's lineage rather quickly. They were wiped out by the Flood, but it popped up again as people kept rejecting God. Pagans around the time of Christ didn't make Christmas, as they didn't care much for Christ anyway.

Instead, they had a holiday of their own near the winter solstice which was likely based on a previous event in their history. (Most holidays go back to some event in the past — Passover and Thanksgiving, for example.) This was a pagan celebration called Saturnalia,[1] which was the Roman festival honoring their god, Saturn.[2] It ran from about December 17–23. However, Saturn was merely the Roman equivalent of the Greek god Cronus/Ceres/Kronos (also known as Kittim or Cethimus).

As you can tell by the dates, it did not overlap with the date used for Christmas (December 25). So any aligning of these two different things requires some speculation. But let's consider Saturn for a moment.

SATURN/CRONUS GOES BACK TO A BIBLE PERSON The land of Greece was inhabited by the descendants of Noah's grandson Javan. In fact, the Hebrew name for Greece is still *Javan*. Javan had four sons, and they were: Elishah, Tarshish (Tarsus), Kittim (Cethimus), and Rodanim (Dodanim).

In Greece and the surrounding area, these names are still a reflection on the landscape. Many of Javan's sons' names and variants have cities, islands, and other geographical features named after them. Paul, the biblical author of two-thirds of

Many of the characters of Greek mythology are based on real historical figures who were raised up to god-like status. One example here is "Hellen," the alleged mythological patriarch and god of the Aeolians (or Elisians). Hellen (Ἕλλην) is likely a variant of Elishah.[3] Even in other cultures, ancestors were often deified; for example, in Germanic and Norse mythologies there is Tiras (Tyras, Tiwaz, Tyr), who was the king of the gods and also happens to be one of Noah's grandsons (Genesis 10:2).

So it makes sense that Cronus/Kronos (Κρόνος), a variant of Cethimas/Kittem, could have been raised up to god-like status. Considering that Noah and his early descendants were living such long lives, it should

the New Testament came from "Tarsus," a variant of Tarshish, though Paul was a Jew who was born and living in this portion of Greece (which gave him citizenship in the Roman Empire; Acts 22:28-29). There were also the "Taurus" mountains in Turkey, and "Tanais" is the old name for the Don River flowing into the Black Sea.

Eliseans was the old name of the ancient Greek tribe now called the Aeolians. Cethimus inhabited the island Cethima, from which the name of the island Cyprus was derived. The name of Cyprus in Hebrew is *Kittiy*, from Kittim. (Josephus, a Jewish historian about 2,000 years ago, elaborated on these relationships in more detail.)

be obvious why many of these ancestors were raised up to be "god-like." Not only did they live long lives, but they were obviously the oldest people around and would seem to be the people (gods, demigods) that started civilization.

Noah would have been roughly 500 years older than anyone else and his sons approximately 100 years older. We know this was because of the Flood, but the true message would quickly be changed to fit the pagan ideas. Thus it is interesting that this pagan festival was likely born as a result of a suppressed view of a biblical character.

Interestingly, this name varia-tion is strikingly similar to bib-lical Kittim/Chittim from whom Cyprus, Kition (now Larnaka, and Josephus gave the name Cethimus 2,000 years ago) get their names. These are all places near Greece, Cyprus, and East-ern Turkey, where Javan's de-scendants came from. Kittim's descendants settled in parts of Eastern Turkey, and Greece and Cyprus. Many old names still bear resemblance to variations of Kittim's name in that region of the world. Kittim was the son of Javan, the son of Japheth (like-ly where the god *Jupiter* comes from), the son of Noah. When Kittim and his family left Babel they settled in these regions.

Like many of the Norse gods, they went back to people in history who were raised up to a god-like status. Considering that Japheth, Javan, and Kittim, etc. often outlived their off-spring with the declining long ages they lived (sometimes 300 to 500 years old), it makes sense why such people were idol-ized and raised up to god-like status. Many pagan cultures have ancestor worship going back to such people who have been "dei-fied" such as Shinto, Norse, Sax-on, and Germanic tribes, as well as Greeks and Romans, etc.

Whether Christmas happens to occur at the same time (or close to the same time) as a pagan

Paganism flourishing today at Christmas

holiday is irrelevant. There is nothing inherently wrong with celebrating a Christian holiday at the same time the pagans celebrate. Do Christians refuse to take communion if it falls on a predominantly pagan holiday like Halloween? Absolutely not. On Halloween, some celebrate Reformation Day, because of what Martin Luther did. Many would contend that Easter is based on ancient pagan holidays, as well, but even if the timing is close to these spring holidays, we remember it because Christ's Resurrection occurred around that time.

What should be of greater concern to Christians is the extent to which we have adopted some of the pagan practices during Christmastime. Some have gone overboard on this, and we should be cautious of making Christmas about mythical images like Santa, Charlie Brown, Rudolph, etc., rather than the birth of Christ and why He came to save those who were lost.

The Church has often failed during Christmastime because we simply talk about the birth of Christ without talking about *why* He came. What is important is that we understand the implication of the omnipotent Son of God leaving His heavenly throne to empty Himself! Why would the Creator of the universe choose to do this, knowing He would be raised by sinful parents in a sinful world to be rejected and to die a horrible death? Unbelievable as it is, it was to pay the penalty for the sin of humankind (Romans 3:23, 6:23) so that we — undeserving, hateful sinners, doomed to die — could instead live with Him in paradise for eternity. Now that is worth celebrating!

(Endnotes)

1   This is not be confused with a Sol Invictus, a day of worship to a Roman state-supported sun god. This began around A.D. 274, well after other dates previously mentioned for Christmas.
2   We use "god(s)" in lower case to refer to the "gods" of mythologies; it is not giving an endorsement of these as "gods." There is only one God, the triune God of Scripture. Note the sixth planet is named for Saturn.
3   Set spellings of names were not necessarily common until recent times. Various languages often had variant spellings of the same name — even same language cultures often had variant spellings. We even see this in the Bible with Jeconiah or Jehoiachin; Xerxes and Ahasuerus.

CHAPTER 5

When *was* Jesus Born?

This is a great question. When we turn to the Scriptures (Luke 1:26–37), it says: *Now in the* **sixth month** *the angel Gabriel was sent by God to a city of Galilee named Nazareth, to a virgin betrothed to a man whose name was Joseph, of the house of David. The virgin's name was Mary. And having come in, the angel said to her, "Rejoice, highly favored one, the Lord is with you; blessed are you among women!"*

But when she saw him, she was troubled at his saying, and considered what manner of greeting this was. Then the angel said to her, "Do not be afraid, Mary, for you have found favor with God. And behold, you will conceive in your womb and bring forth a Son, and shall call His name Jesus. He will be great, and will be called the Son of the Highest; and the Lord God will give Him the throne of His father David. And He will reign over the house of Jacob forever, and of His kingdom there will be no end."

Then Mary said to the angel, "How can this be, since I do not know a man?"

And the angel answered and said to her, "The Holy Spirit will come upon you, and the power of the Highest will overshadow you; therefore, also, that Holy One who is to be born will be called the Son of God. Now indeed, Elizabeth your relative has also conceived a son in her old age; and this is now the **sixth month** *for her who was called barren. For with God nothing will be impossible"* (emphasis added).

Here we learn approximately when John was conceived, relative to when the Holy Spirit came upon Mary for the conception of Christ. John would have been conceived around six months before Jesus. If we assume John's conception was the previous year's final month or perhaps the first month of the year, we can do some rough calculations. By assuming this, Elizabeth, John's mother, could have been in her sixth month during the sixth month of the Jewish year.

In Witness Whereof the said

caused this Certificate to be

thorized offic

23

This meeting with Gabriel was presumably close to the time when the Holy Spirit would come upon Mary. In fact, it could have been almost immediate, as verse 28 indicates *"the Lord is with you,"* but it was likely soon after, as verse 35 says *"will come upon you."*

In the Jewish calendar, there are 12 months of roughly 30 days each with a leap month every so often to get them back to about 365 days.

Jewish calendar equivalents

MONTH	NAME	SCRIPTURE REFERENCE	MODERN GREGORIAN CALENDAR EQUIVALENT
First	Nisan	Esther 3:7	March–April
Second	Iyar (Iyyar)	N/A	April–May
Third	Sivan	Esther 8:9	May–June
Fourth	Tammuz	N/A	June–July
Fifth	Ab (Av)	N/A	July–August
Sixth	Elul	Nehemiah 6:15	August–September
Seventh	Tishri	N/A	September–October
Eighth	Marchesvan (Heshvan)	N/A	October–November
Ninth	Chislev (Kislev)	Nehemiah 1:1; Zechariah 7:1	November–December
Tenth	Tebet (Tevet)	Esther 2:16	December–January
Eleventh	Sheni (Shevat)	N/A	January–February
Twelfth	Adar	Esther 3:7, 9:1	February–March
Leap month (intercalary)	Adar Sheni (second Adar)	N/A	February–March on leap years

This would have put John the Baptist at about six months in the womb around August/September. Assuming about nine months for pregnancy, John would have been born about November/December by the modern calendar, based on the assumptions we used.

If the Holy Spirit did come upon Mary in the sixth month (Elul) or around August/September, then Jesus should have been born about nine months later, which would place His birth around May/June. Since John the Baptist was still in the womb of Elizabeth when he leapt for joy in Jesus' presence (Luke 1:39-42), this means that the conception had to take place within the next three months or so of the visit by Gabriel — before John was born. Regardless, by this reckoning, the birth of Christ isn't even close to Christmas on the modern calendar.

Be still, and know that I am God;
I will be exalted among the nations,
I will be exalted in the earth!

— Psalm 46:10

OTHER NEW YEAR'S DAYS ON THE JEWISH CALENDAR?

We need to exercise some caution since we were using some assumptions (e.g., no leap month and the date of the Jewish New Year. Esther 3:7 points out that Nisan is the first month of the Jewish calendar, and that is still acknowledged today. In Judaism, however, there are other "new year's" days as well. The most popular is called Rosh Hashanah, literally meaning "head of the year."

Rosh Hashanah is celebrated on the first of Tishri, which is normally the 7th month (Leviticus 23:24) and is the start of the civil year. If this were the reference point for the news when the angel Gabriel met Mary, then the 6th month from this would have been the 12th month on the normal Jewish calendar (or February/March), and if this were the case, then Jesus would have been born nine months later in November/December. So it is not without biblical merit that December may have been the date of Christ's birth if we use Rosh Hashanah as the start of the new year.

Around A.D. 220 Julius Africanus, an early Christian writer, reckoned that Jesus was conceived on March 25.[1] Hence, nine months later — about December 25 — Jesus was born. Other Christians have made cases for the December Christmastime as well. Ultimately, we can't know exactly when He was born.

To clarify some points, we, nor other Christians, do not "worship" a pagan holiday or any holiday. We "worship" God on the day that is set aside as Christmas. We take time to "remember" (not worship) the birth of Christ on that day. This is important, because we often get wrapped up in the wrong things, and sometimes we need to step back and remember: *Be still, and know that I am God; I will be exalted among the nations, I will be exalted in the earth* (Psalm 46:10).

ZACHARIAS AND THE FEAST OF TABERNACLES

Some have cleverly reckoned that *if* we can find out the time when Zacharias (John the Baptist's father) was serving at the temple, then we can find approximate dates for both John the Baptist's and Jesus' births (since they should be about six months apart). Logically, this is a sound argument, and it has potential.

If we jump back to Temple service in the time of David the King, he was preparing for aspects of the Temple for Solomon would build (as the Lord would not permit David to build it). But David did make preparations and even began the divisions of priests to work the temple at allotted schedules (1 Chronicles 28:13).

These divisions for service were broken down previously in Chronicles (1 Chronicles 24:1–19). They were of the order of Aaron and his four sons (Nadab, Abihu, Eleazar, and Ithamar). Of course, two of Aaron's sons had died without children (Nadab and Abihu). So all 24 divisions came from Eleazar and Ithamar, and since Eleazar has more children, they accordingly had more divisions.

Each division had to work the temple over the course of a week from a Sabbath to Sabbath (2 Chronicles 23:8). Then it is

And the order of service is listed below:

Name/Division

1. Jehoiarib
2. Jedaiah
3. Harim
4. Seorim
5. Malchijah
6. Mijamin
7. Hakkoz
8. Abijah
9. Jeshua
10. Shecaniah
11. Eliashib
12. Jakim
13. Huppah
14. Jeshebeab
15. Bilgah
16. Immer
17. Hezir
18. Happizzez
19. Pethahiah
20. Jehezekel
21. Jachin
22. Gamul
23. Delaiah
24. Maaziah

assumed that service began on the first Sabbath on the first month of the Jewish calendar (Nisan or March/April), hence Zacharias who was in the eighth order of Abijah or Abia (Luke 1:5) would have been around May/June, and six month later Jesus would have been conceived around November/December, and accordingly was born about nine months later in August/September. On top of this, we do know that shepherds were outside with their flocks at night so it may have been a bit warmer, too, so this makes sense.

OBJECTIONS TO SERVICE RECKONING Although this sounds good at first, but we still need to exercise some caution unless there is more information presented. What stuck out was the assumption that the priestly order of service began at the *first month*. The Bible was silent on this, and for good reasons. It makes more sense that temple service began when the temple was complete [initially during the reign of Solomon]: *And in the eleventh year, in the month of Bul, which is the eighth month, the house was finished in all its details and according to all its plans. So he was seven years in building it* (1 Kings 6:38).

It seems unlikely that service to the temple would be put off for several months, but instead began in the month of Bul, which is the eighth month. But as the Old Testament reveals, many Israelites fell short of God's expectation and services surely fell short. Recall Hezekiah having to renovate the temple and get the Levites back on track in 2 Chronicles 29.

Notice another problem — the month of Bul does not appear on the current Jewish calendar. In fact, the Bible refers to other months in the time of Moses up to the captivity. (Prior to Moses, in the days of Noah the months were simply given as numbers, not names, so this development is most likely a post-Flood development.) Moses was aware of the system of months with names as he later mentioned the month of **Abib** in Exodus 13:4, 23:15, 34:18, and Deuteronomy 16:1. Other months were also mentioned later than Moses such as **Ziv** in 1 Kings 6:1 and 6:37; **Ethanim** in 1 Kings 8:2; and, of course, **Bul** in 1 Kings 6:38.

These four months mentioned correspond to the ancient Canaanite months and refer to agriculturally significant months for their etymology.[2] For example, Abib means *"the month when barley shoots into an ear,"* and so on. This Canaanite influence is to be expected considering that Abraham moved and lived among the Canaanites as did his descendants for many years, prior to moving to Egypt and Moses bringing them back to the land of Canaan, which was the Promised Land.

Furthermore, the Jewish calendar that we are familiar with (and uses Nisan as the first month) is virtually identical to the Babylonian calendar, and rightly so. The Jews borrowed that calendar when they were in captivity in Babylon. This is why references to that calendar do not appear in the Bible until Esther and Nehemiah, which

were after the captivity (Nisan - Esther 3:7, Sivan - Esther 8:9, Elul - Nehemiah 6:15, Tebet - Esther 2:16, Adar - Esther 3:7, and Adar - Esther 9:1). So the question really is, how could they begin their service in the month of Nisan when that calendar was not in use among the Israelites yet?

Fast-forwarding in time, after the captivity Ezra 6:18 records the reassignment of the priestly divisions. But there was a problem. Not all the divisions returned for service. Dr. John Gill points out in his commentary on 1 Chronicles 24:7:

. . . . the Jews say only four of these courses returned from the Babylonish captivity, which were those of Jedaiah, Harim, Pashur, and Immer; though Pashur is not among these here; yet they say each of these four had six lots, and that the names and the order of the other courses were retained and continued under them.[3]

We know that Zacharias in Luke 1:5 was of Abijah (or at least performed the duties of that service time), so that specific lineage had to have been reassigned. In fact, there is no reason to assume that all 24 divisions were not reassigned since they did this in accordance with the Law of Moses. In keeping with this ordinance, they would have likely kept with the same ordering of the priestly lineage's names.

After the captivity though, the temple needed renovating, etc. Ezra records that the Temple had been completed and ready for service on the third day of the month of Adar (Ezra 6:15). Again, it makes sense that the priestly duties began at this time, with the first division. Because the Bible doesn't give an absolute beginning to the onset of the priestly duties, it may not be wise to assume a date, especially since God knew there would be different completion dates and accordingly different dates to begin service.

It is possible, I suppose, if someone wanted to work out the calculation based on this latest date of initial service, that they may be closer to John's and, likewise, Jesus' birth. But one must also consider Herod's Temple, of which Zacharias was working. According to John 2:20, it was built about 46 years before Jesus' proclamation that He would *raise up the temple in three days.*

When was its exact commission date? Did they start over with the first division of priests? The Bible simply does not tell us. So at this point we can still not be certain of the date of Christ's birth. But we can say that Jesus was born closer to the late evening/night, for an angel informed the shepherds of Christ's birth *at night.*

(Endnotes)

1   Sextus Julius Africanus, Chronographiai, a.d. 221.

2   Jack Finegan, *Handbook of Biblical Chronology, Revised Edition* (Peabody, MA: Hendickson Publishers, 1998), p. 18–64.

3   John Gill, *Exposition of the Entire Bible:* Commentary Note on Luke 1:5 (1748-1763).

CHAPTER 6

Timeline
of Events
Surrounding
Christ's
Birth

Skeptics often dismiss the accounts of Matthew 2 and Luke 2 by claiming they do not line up, and therefore the accounts should be discarded. Sometimes they go so far as to say that few are even aware of these issues.

But is this really a problem? When we take a closer look, this claim is simply reduced to dust. The following is a plausible timeline that makes sense and works well with the information given in the Scriptures.[1]

CIRCA 4 B.C.[2]

a. Because of the Roman census, Joseph and Mary travel to Bethlehem from their hometown of Nazareth. Jesus was likely born in the lower room where animals often stay, not the guest room (*kataluma*), and subsequently laid in a manger (Luke 1:26–27, 2:4–7).

b. The shepherds visited following the angelic announcement (Luke 2:8–12, 20).

c. The angels worshiped the Christ (Luke 2:13–14).

EIGHT DAYS LATER

Jesus was circumcised. This probably did not occur in Jerusalem but a local synagogue or perhaps a priest came to them, as was the case for John the Baptist (Luke 1:59, 2:21; Leviticus 12:3).

Jesus was given His name (Luke 2:21).

AT LEAST 41 DAYS AFTER HIS BIRTH

The Law stipulated a woman wait 40 days following the birth of a son to finish her purification (Leviticus 12:1–8). So Mary and Joseph went to the temple in Jerusalem to offer a sacrifice of two doves or pigeons, which signified they were poor (Luke 2:22–24). This suggests the magi had not visited yet to offer their expensive gifts; otherwise, Joseph and Mary could have afforded the lamb and dove required by the Law for those with adequate means.

At the temple, Simeon held Jesus, blessed God and the family, and prophesied in the Holy Spirit about Jesus (Luke 2:25–35).

Anna, a prophetess, saw the Christ at the temple (Luke 2:36–38).

SOON AFTER THE 41ST DAY

The family returned to Bethlehem — not Nazareth, as some have suggested. After all, they were still in Bethlehem when the wise men later visited and they apparently planned to return there following the flight to Egypt. [3] As such, it is unlikely they would have packed up everything to go to Jerusalem for offering sacrifices. So they would have returned to Bethlehem where they left their belongings (Matthew 2:5–9).

They were now staying in a house (*oikian*) — perhaps the same one, but probably not in the stall area since the guest room (*kataluma*) may have been available at this time.

WITHIN THE YEAR[4]

Alerted by the so-called Christmas star, an unknown number of magi from the East (perhaps Persia[5]) made their way to Herod's palace in Jerusalem to inquire of the Christ child (Matthew 2:1–4).

Contrary to popular opinion, the star was not a typical event in the heavens (e.g., supernova, planetary alignment, comet, etc.) Instead, it was truly a miraculous and special star (Matthew 2:2, 7, 9–11).

Jewish chief priests and scribes informed Herod that, according to Micah 5:2, Bethlehem was to be the birthplace of the Messiah (Matthew 2:4–6).

These magi followed the star, which moved ahead of them, bringing expensive gifts of gold, frankincense, and myrrh to Jesus — who was now a young child living in a house[6] (Matthew 2:9–11).

They worshiped the Christ Child (Matthew 2:11).

Jesus is called a "young Child" (*paidion,* Matthew 2) instead of babe (*brephos,* Luke 2:16) at the time that the magi arrived. *Brephos* specifically refers to a baby, whether born or unborn, while *paidion* refers to an immature child, possibly an infant (Matthew 2:11), so we should not be dogmatic about His age.

They returned to their homeland via a different route after being divinely warned in a dream not to go back to Herod (Matthew 2:12).

Soon after the wise men left, Herod realized that they were not going to return and he ordered the killing of all boys in and around the region of Bethlehem who were two years of age and under (Matthew 2:16). Herod knew the approximate timing of the appearing of the star (Matthew 2:7), which may be the time that Christ was born. With this information, Herod, who was paranoid about the crown and did not want anyone taking over, would have made sure to kill the child. So he may have at least doubled the time from when the star first appeared to the wise men, thinking this would guarantee that the child would be killed, even if the information was off.

An angel warned Joseph to flee to Egypt to protect his family. This trip would ultimately fulfill a prophecy (Hosea 11:1). Perhaps the new gifts helped finance that trip (Matthew 2:13–15).

LATE 4 B.C. TO EARLY 3 B.C.

Herod died in 4 B.C. in Jericho and was buried in Herodion approximately 25 miles away. Reports are that the procession traveled with the body one mile per day. So it was likely 3 B.C. when he was buried.[7] Herod's son Archelaus took over (Matthew 2:22).

EARLY 3 B.C.

An angel informed Joseph that they could move back since Herod had died (Matthew 2:15, 19).

Since Joseph and Mary had completed the laws and commands (*nomos* in Greek) of the Lord, they returned to the land of Israel from Egypt and settled in Nazareth of Galilee, which became the hometown of Jesus and was where Joseph and Mary lived prior to going to Bethlehem for the census[8] (Matthew 2:22; Luke 2:39).

Jesus would be called a Nazarene, fulfilling a spoken prophecy (Matthew 2:23).

Herod's tomb in Herodion (Herodyon, Herodium) Elef Millim project

The timeline makes sense when the Gospels of Luke and Matthew are carefully analyzed. Any alleged contradiction of the timeline at the time of Christ's entrance into the world simply vanishes in light of the chronology given. When it comes to the Scriptures, they can be trusted. Sometimes we just need to take some time to carefully study them.

And the Child grew and became strong in spirit, filled with wisdom; and the grace of God was upon Him.
—Luke 2:40

(Endnotes)

1   We should not be dogmatic about the specific details here. This article is designed to show that the details of the biblical account are not contradictory but entirely consistent.

2   Ussher believed Jesus was born near the beginning of 4 B.C. since the king, Herod the Great, died near the end of that year, and Jesus was born during his reign. James Ussher, translated by Larry and Marion Pierce, *The Annals of the World* (Green Forest, AR: Master Books, 2003), p. 779.

3   Some respected chronologists place the visit of the magi, the flight to Egypt, Herod's death, and the return from Egypt prior to Mary's sacrifices on the 40th day at the temple. See Dr. Floyd Jones, *Chronology of the Old Testament* (Green Forest, AR: Master Books, 2005), p. 214–216. Though this is possible, there are some problems. For example, Matthew 2:21–22 states: "Then he arose, took the young Child and His mother, and came into the land of Israel. But when he heard that Archelaus was reigning over Judea instead of his father Herod, he was afraid to go there. And being warned by God in a dream, he turned aside into the region of Galilee." Why would Joseph take Mary and Jesus to the temple *in Jerusalem* when they feared Archelaus (Herod's son) who was ruling in Jerusalem? Why would they go to Judea after being instructed by an angel to go to Galilee?

4   Ussher places the visit of the magi prior to the 40th day (*The Annals of the World*, p. 779). Some churches celebrate the Epiphany on January 6 (12 days after Christmas) in honor of the visit of the magi. This is the origin of the "12 days of Christmas" tradition. However, it makes more sense that Joseph and Mary were still poor. Furthermore, they were likely still living with relatives during the census period and potentially in the same animal-housing portion of the place where Jesus was born and laid in a manger. It was not until later that they were living in a house when the wise men visited.

5   The magi may have been familiar with the promises of the coming Messiah due to Daniel's influence and/or the Jewish holdovers from the Babylonian captivity. The Hebrew scrolls (e.g., Numbers 24:17) would have been highly revered among magi. Keep in mind that magi and wise men were together among the elite in Babylon in those days. Daniel 2:48 states that Daniel was elevated above all of them.

6   Some may propose that Joseph, Mary, and Jesus were in Nazareth already and the star then altered the magi's journey from Bethlehem to Nazareth. However, if this were the case, then there would have been no reason for the angel to warn Joseph to flee to Egypt to avoid the coming massacre by Herod. Had they moved to Nazareth immediately after doing business in Jerusalem and did not return to Bethlehem where they had been staying, they would have had to arrive back in Bethlehem for the visit from the magi. So it still makes more sense to have them go back to Bethlehem after the sacrifices.

7   Josephus, *Antiquity of the Jews*, Book 17, chapter 8 [Herod's death — his last will — burial. 4, 3 B.C.] and *Wars of the Jews*, Book 1, chapter 33 [The golden eagle cut to pieces — Herod's barbarity — attempts to kill himself — commands Antipater to be slain — survives him by five days. 4 B.C.] *The Revised Works of Josephus*). See also Ussher, *The Annals of the World*, p. 781.

8   Luke 2:39 indicates that when they had completed all that was required of them by the Lord, they returned and settled in Galilee where they had originally come from. This would have been upon their return from Egypt to complete what had been stated by the Lord through the angels. They had completed the temple rituals given by Moses, and they had now just completed the instructions given by an angel to leave and return. Their decision to go to Galilee was prompted by an angel due to Herod's son Archelaus taking the reign in Judea because Galilee was out of his jurisdiction (Matthew 2:22).

CHAPTER 7

Making the
Christmas Sermon
Relevant for Today's
Culture

If you think that the average "Christmas message" doesn't move non-believers, you're not alone. This might help some pastors reach more.

I heard several sermons on the birth of Jesus. Now, in our Western culture that is rapidly losing its once-Christian worldview, Christians and Christian leaders need to use this time more than ever to challenge non-Christians. But will they give the vital message people need to hear at this time of history?

I was thrilled to be able to bring a friend who has struggled with the Christian faith for his entire life to church one Christmas season. Just before we arrived, he asked me a question that had been troubling him. I was fascinated to note that he didn't ask about Jesus and the manger, or about the shepherds or the angels who proclaimed the birth of Jesus on earth — instead, he asked, "Why do many Christians use organ transplants to prolong their life or try to prolong the lives of their children when they're born with problems and God had deemed it was their time to die?" He continued, "Why wouldn't a Christian accept their death that came from God? Shouldn't they just accept it if they are true Christians and want to go to heaven instead of trying to survive on this earth?"

Now, why would he ask questions like that? The answer is that the culture is increasingly losing the true meaning of Christmas because the education system and the media continues to indoctrinate people to reject the Bible as absolute truth. Instead, the Christian faith and the Bible is attacked, ridiculed, and condemned as a "book of stories" because so-called science has supposedly proved it cannot be true — particularly its history in Genesis.

I'm sure my friend wasn't expecting an answer. After all, such questions as the ones he asked have been leveled at Christians for years. (Sadly, many Christians don't know how to answer such questions,

The last enemy that will be destroyed is death.
— I Corinthians 15:26

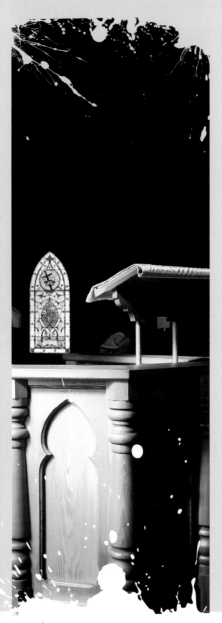

because they, like him, don't believe the true history of the world from Genesis — which explains the origin and meaning of death.)

I was sure the sermon we were about to hear would be from a pastor who assumed people believed the Bible. I thought he would remind them of the babe in a manger and why He came to earth. I realized that my friend needed answers, so he would know that he could trust the Bible before he even heard the sermon. I was pleased he had asked me what was on his heart, a question that was one of things stopping him from considering the Christian faith.

My friend had viewed death, suffering, and dying as something God must be responsible for — which was the crux of the issue. He did not understand that death was an enemy (1 Corinthians 15:26), an intrusion due to sin. Death wasn't something that God made and declared *very good* in Genesis 1:31, but a result of sin. I explained that God created a *perfect* world, and because the first man Adam sinned, death entered the world as the punishment for sin. I had to explain that the earth was not millions of years old as he had been indoctrinated to believe, and thus there was not death, disease, and bloodshed for millions of

years before man's existence.

I continued: When man sinned, God as a righteous and holy Creator had to judge sin with death. It was as if He withdrew some of His sustaining power to *no longer* uphold the universe in a perfect state to cause man to experience a taste of what happens without God. Thus, God is permitting things like disease and suffering, to happen, but He isn't the one to blame for this — man is. Then it was like a light bulb came on in my friend's head. With this new view of God, the Bible started to make sense to him.

Sadly, there are many people within the Church who accept the supposed millions of years, instead of the truth as given in Genesis. Because of this, they don't have valid answers for people like my friend, but instead would ignore his questions and relate the story of the babe in the manger in the hope my friend would start believing this.

Many people struggle with accepting the truth of Jesus and the Bible because they have the wrong view of history. They, like my friend, have been indoctrinated to reject the Bible as a true account of history and the meaning of life. This is a major stumbling block for so many people to believing God's Word and being saved.

Knowing that many non-Christians view God like this and also knowing that they only set foot in church about once a year, I'm praying that Christian leaders will take advantage of this opportunity and address issues like *death and suffering, and how we know the Bible is true, dinosaurs,* and so on, that are relevant issues for where the culture is today, while speaking during this Christmas season. This could make such a difference in the lives of many who have a faulty view of God, and thus challenge them concerning the truth of the Bible.

And I will put enmity between you and the woman, and between your seed and her Seed; He shall bruise your head, and you shalt bruise His heel.

—Genesis 3:15

FOUNDATION OF CHRISTMAS

In one sermon that I heard, the minister said "Let's turn in the Bible to the foundation of Christmas." Then he said to go to Luke chapter 2. I immediately thought to myself, *That's not the foundation of Christmas. That **was** the first Christmas.*

The foundation of Christmas goes back much further. It starts in the first book of the Bible — Genesis. The initial reference to the birth of Jesus is in Genesis 3:15.

And I will put enmity between you and the woman, and between your seed and her Seed; He shall bruise your head, and you shalt bruise His heel (Genesis 3:15).

This first prophecy pointing to the virgin birth of Jesus (seed of a woman) came immediately after Adam and Eve sinned. Though they were sentenced to die, God in His mercy gave a promise of redemption through the one who would be born of a virgin as Isaiah further elaborates — Jesus Christ (Isaiah 7:14).

In fact, many references to Jesus' birth have their foundation in Genesis, such as Jesus being a descendant of Isaac (Genesis 26:4) and Jacob (Genesis 28:13–14). Ultimately, the foundation of Jesus' birth goes back to Genesis. This is where a Christmas sermon should start — particularly in a culture that has been brainwashed to believe that part of the Bible cannot possibly be true. Why would these people listen to a sermon about Bethlehem, the stable, the shepherds, and the wise men if they already think the book it all comes from cannot be trusted.

Genesis is where we first learn about the *bad news* of Adam's sin that allowed death to enter into the creation. In today's culture, people continually preach the *good news* of Jesus but fail to teach the bad news in Genesis. This is why many don't listen to the good news because they failed to understand the bad

news in Genesis.

We need to teach people to understand *why* they need Jesus before they'll understand their need to receive Jesus. They need a proper foundation — they need to be taken back to Genesis and first of all be taught that modern science has not disproved this historical document but actually confirms it. Then they need to be taught the foundational truths of Genesis that enable one to understand what the babe in a manger is all about.

WHY JESUS HAD TO BE BORN

Back in Genesis, the bad news of Adam's sin was punishable by death (Genesis 2:17). Romans 6:23 confirms that the wages of sin is death. Adam and Eve sinned, so something had to die to cover that sin. This is why God killed animals to cover Adam and Eve's sin (Genesis 3:21). Although we don't know what animals were sacrificed, we have often pictured it as a lamb foreshadowing the Gospel. Jesus, the Lamb of God, was the final sacrifice to cover peoples' sins on the Cross.

The Israelites followed this pattern by presenting sin offerings to cover their sins by sacrificing an animal life for their disobedience to God. But an animal can't take away the sin of a man, as humans are not related to any other creature — man was made in the image of God.

God is a God of grace. When someone rightly decrees punishment to someone for their crime, then, out of love, takes that punishment upon themselves; that's grace and mercy. This is why our Creator, in the person of Jesus Christ, had to come into the world — He became a human (but remained God) so He could pay the ultimate penalty for our sin.

God sentenced man to death because of our sin. He showed His love for us by exercising grace and took the punishment upon Himself. Jesus, being God, came into the world just like any other person — by being born. Yet Jesus lived a perfect life so that He could be the final sacrifice to cover all peoples' sins. This is why Jesus was born and why Jesus had to die. This is why Jesus is called *the last Adam* (1 Corinthians 15:45) — He in effect became a "new Adam," a "perfect Adam," so He could die for the descendants of Adam and offer them a free gift of salvation.

The Bible says the greatest act of love is when one lays down his life for his friends (John 15:13). The God of the Bible displays this kind of love.

WAS JESUS REALLY BORN OF A VIRGIN? Isaiah also predicted that a virgin would bear a child and this would be a sign.

Then he said, "Hear now, O house of David! Is it a small thing for you to weary men, but will you weary my God also? Therefore the Lord Himself will give you a sign: Behold, the virgin shall conceive and bear a Son, and shall call His name Immanuel (Isaiah 7:13–14).

These prophecies were manifested in Mary, a virgin. She delivered a baby boy who was called Immanuel — meaning "God with us." Besides, Joseph couldn't be the father of Jesus! The genealogy of Joseph in Matthew 1:1–16 yields that Jeconiah (variation of Jehoiachin) was a direct ancestor of Joseph.

Why is this significant? Please read the curse given to Jehoiachin from Jeremiah: *Thus says the* LORD: *'Write this man down as childless, A man who shall not prosper in his days; For none of his descendants shall prosper, Sitting on the throne of David, And ruling anymore in Judah'"* (Jeremiah 22:30).

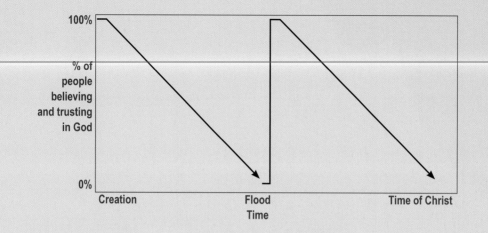

% of people believing and trusting in God

Creation — Flood — Time of Christ

Time

Jesus, sitting forever on the throne of David, could not have been Jehoiachin's descendant since no descendant of Jeconiah, thus descendant of Joseph, could inherit the throne of David. Therefore, Mary had to be a virgin. Isaiah confirms that Jesus will reign on the throne of David.

Of the increase of His government and peace there will be no end, Upon the throne of David and over His kingdom, to order it and establish it with judgment and justice from that time forward, even forever. The zeal of the Lord of hosts will perform this (Isaiah 9:7).

SIGNIFICANCE OF BABY JESUS Jesus' entrance into the world was fascinating! Fulfilling prophecy, having gifts brought from afar, having local shepherd men honor him, having a king attempt to assassinate him (Jeremiah 31:15 and Matthew 2:16–18) and fleeing to Egypt in the middle of the night (Matthew 2:13–15) were a few miracles that hint at the importance of this child.

For unto us a Child is born, unto us a Son is given; and the government will be upon His shoulder. And His name will be called Wonderful, Counselor, Mighty God, Everlasting Father, Prince of Peace (Isaiah 9:6).

God, the Son, left His sanctuary to be made lesser in the form of a human. He left behind heavenly perfection to live as one of us. This child restored the broken relationship, due to Adam's sin in Genesis 3, between man and God.

For there is born to you this day in the city of David a Savior, who is Christ the Lord (Luke 2:11).

Jesus came to earth at a very significant point in earth history, too. Let's consider the past and get the big picture of this significance. (See the graph.)

In Genesis, when Adam and Eve were the only people on earth, 100 percent of the people believed and trusted in God

(albeit they become sinners). As time progressed, people stopped believing and trusting in God.

In Genesis at the time of Noah, his family was the only ones on earth that still believed and trusted in God enough to enter the ark. So the percentage was rather low considering the population had continued to grow.

After God sent the Flood, Noah's family was the only one on earth, so the percentage was again nearly 100 percent of people believing and trusting in God.

As time progressed, God kept calling the Israelites back to Him. Ultimately, though, as the population of the earth re-grew, the overall percentage began to drop. Just before Jesus' birth the bulk of the world's people were not believing or trusting in God.

Even the Pharisees, Jewish leaders in the time of Jesus, were not trusting in God but following traditions and not what God was actually saying in the Bible — otherwise they would have been expecting the Messiah.

The wise men knew, and John the Baptist, who prepared many in Israel for Jesus, knew. This is still a very low percentage of people believing and trusting in God when Jesus was born. Jesus came when few believed and trusted in God.

When Jesus came to earth it was a low point in earth history, so His timing was very significant, but the mission was completed perfectly and we now have the opportunity to return to God as a free gift in Jesus Christ.

So hopefully the next Christmas sermon you hear will incorporate some of the answers that people need in today's culture. When you answer questions people have about the trustworthiness of the Bible they will be more open to the gospel itself, which is also found in the pages of the Bible.

Confusion

······ *and* ······

Happy Holidays!

Misconceptions

CHAPTER 8

Misconceptions

Surrounding

Christmas

—

An Introduction

Answers in Genesis is a ministry devoted to biblical authority. This means that we believe the Bible is the inspired, inerrant, and authoritative Word of God. The Bible can be trusted from the very first verse, and it must be the basis for our thinking.

One of the keys to taking a stand on the Word of God is making sure we understand what is actually stated in the Bible. Too often we allow other sources to influence our thinking about certain Bible passages. Christians must learn to be serious students of the Word. We need to pay close attention to the text itself rather than allowing our culture and traditions to determine our understanding.

Many of us have been led to believe that the Bible proclaims some things it really doesn't. This is often the result of well-intentioned but inaccurate teaching in Sunday school, sermons, songs, portrayals of biblical accounts in film and television, or even our own misinterpretation of the Bible.

Nowhere are these misconceptions more apparent than in our understanding of the birth of Christ. The little drummer boy, Santa Claus, Frosty the Snowman, and Rudolph the Red-nosed Reindeer have nothing to do with that night over 2,000 years ago when the Lord Jesus Christ was born, yet they have become part of our culture's portrayal of Christmas. When we, as Christians, are careless with our reading of the text, it is easy to become guilty of embellishing the accounts.

While these misconceptions are usually unintentional, we must still be careful not to add or subtract from God's Word. We pray that the lessons here will help you pay closer attention as you read and study His Word, and that you will come to a deeper and more accurate understanding of the Bible.

A new born King to see,
pa rum pum pum pum

CHAPTER 9

The X Stands for Christ

THE X STANDS FOR CHRIST

We've all seen the signs wishing people a Merry Xmas. What does the X stand for in Xmas? How can some claim that the X stands for Christ, while others say that this is another attempt at removing Christ from the culture? Which view is correct? In a sense, both are.

Christ is a title given to the Lord Jesus to signify that He is the Messiah. In Greek, this word is Christos (χριστος). Since the first Greek letter of this title (the letter *chi*) looks like an x in English, some have used it as an abbreviation for Christ.[1] Many have claimed that this practice dates back to the first century, and there is solid evidence that shows this was practiced in the 16th century, perhaps as a cost-saving measure for those using the printing press. However, those using the abbreviation would still pronounce the X as Christ.

There is no question that many use the X today for the very purpose of eliminating Christ from the holiday that bears His title. Some may even do this in ignorance. Secularists have been working hard to remove any mention of God, Jesus, and Christianity from our culture. Should we expect anything less from those who don't know the Lord?

So what is a Christian to do? Can we use the abbreviation or must we always write out Christmas? I believe one needs to follow his or her own conscience, guided by the Holy Spirit, on this issue — as with every other. It is not sinful to use abbreviations, but it would definitely be wrong for a Christian to use it because he or she is ashamed of Jesus Christ (Luke 9:26). As such, one must examine his or her reasons for whatever decision they reach.

(Endnotes)

1   The chi-rho abbreviation, formed by a combination of the first two letters in Christ (looks like a blending of x and p), was common in the early Church, and was eventually adopted as an official symbol by Constantine.

CHAPTER 10

We Three Kings

Nativity scenes around the world display them. Songs and poems have been written about them. They are featured in movies, plays, and Sunday school skits. They are some of the most recognizable figures in our culture as nearly everyone has seen images of three wise men riding on camels and following a star. Some have even gone so far as to name these guys.

What do we really know about these men, now known as Gaspar, Melchior, and Balthasar? Does the biblical account of the magi support the traditional story surrounding these enigmatic characters? This section will examine many of the details given in Scripture concerning the magi. Who were they? How did they learn about the King of the Jews? How many were there? When and where did they see the Lord Jesus Christ?

MAGI, KINGS, OR WISE MEN? The Greek word μαγοι (mágoi) is translated as "wise men" in the NKJV, KJV, and ESV, while the NASB and NIV use the word "magi." Originally, the word often referred to a class of Persian wise men, and possibly priests, who were interpreters of special signs, particularly in astrology (see Daniel 2:1–18). Eventually, the word was used variously to refer to one who possessed supernatural knowledge and ability, a magician, or even a deceiver or seducer.[1] There is little to no New Testament basis for identifying them as kings.[2]

The Book of Matthew contains the account of the wise men:

Now after Jesus was born in Bethlehem of Judea in the days of Herod the king, behold, wise men from the East came to Jerusalem, saying "Where is He who has been born King of the Jews? For we have seen His star in the East and have come to worship Him" (Matthew 2:1–2).

The original meaning of *mágoi* is likely in view here — wise men who interpreted special signs. There are at least three reasons for this identification.

First, they acknowledged that they were interested in signs in the heavens. Second, the Bible states that they were from "the East," which would be in the direction of Babylon and ancient Persia.[3] Third, of all the peoples of "the East," the Babylonians, had many opportunities to learn of the Jewish Scriptures, which contain multiple promises of the coming Messiah. Daniel was an influential government official in Babylon about 600 years earlier, and he foretold the coming of the Messiah (Daniel 9:24–26). Also, tens of thousands of Jews lived in Babylon during the time of the exile (605–536 B.C.), and they maintained a large presence there for the following centuries.

HOW DID THEY LEARN OF THE KING OF THE JEWS?

The third reason above provides a plausible solution to this question. Since the magi presumably had access to the Hebrew Scriptures, they could have known about the promises of the coming Messiah. Some scholars believe that the Book of Numbers informed the magi of the child who would be preceded by a star. *I see Him, but not now; I behold Him, but not near; a Star shall come out of Jacob; a Scepter shall rise out of Israel* (Numbers 24:17). Perhaps they were told in a dream about the Messiah's birth. After all, God warned them in a dream not to return to Herod

after they had seen the baby Jesus and presented their gifts to Him (Matthew 2:12).

While these are both plausible suggestions, we do not have enough information about the magi to know for sure. However, we can be sure that they fully expected to behold a child who was "born King of the Jews." This is probably why they traveled first to Jerusalem, the most likely location for the birth of a Jewish king.

HOW MANY MAGI CAME TO SEE JESUS?
Although the popular Christmas hymn and traditions tell us that three wise men visited Christ, the Bible does not give us the number of wise men. Matthew wrote the following concerning the magi's visit:

When they heard the king, they departed; and behold, the star which they had seen in the East went before them, till it came and stood over where the young Child was. When they saw the star, they rejoiced with exceedingly great joy. And when they had come into the house, they saw the young Child with Mary His mother, and fell down and worshiped Him. And when they had opened their treasures, they presented gifts to Him: gold, frankincense, and myrrh (Matthew 2:9–11).

The traditional view that three wise men journeyed to see Christ is likely based on the fact that three gifts were given. However, since the Bible does not tell us the number of magi, we can only speculate. We know there were at least two magi, and there may have been many more.

WHEN AND WHERE DID THEY SEE THE LORD JESUS CHRIST?
The traditional view presented in films, such as The Nativity Story, is that the wise men saw Jesus on the night of His birth, but this is highly unlikely. Matthew 2:1 reveals that the magi came to Jerusalem and subsequently visited with Herod after Jesus had been born.

The angelic announcement of Christ's birth to the shepherds was at night, which means that Jesus was born at night. In Luke 2:11, the angel told the shep-

CHAPTER 11

HARK!
The Herald
Angels Said?

Sing it with me. "Hark! The herald angels sing, 'Glory to the newborn King! Peace on earth and mercy mild, God and sinners reconciled.'"

Most of us are familiar with this beloved Christmas carol, written by Charles Wesley, which tells of an angelic chorus singing praises to God. In fact, many of our favorite Christmas hymns portray angels singing following the announcement of Christ's birth to the shepherds, including "It Came Upon a Midnight Clear," "O Little Town of Bethlehem," and "Silent Night."

The idea of an angelic chorus singing praises to God has become very common in our culture. Many churches depict it in their annual Christmas programs. Even Charles Spur-geon, the famous 19th-century preacher, waxed eloquent on singing angels:

And notice how well they told the story, and surely you will love them! Not with the stammering tongue of one who tells a tale in which he has no interest; nor even with the feigned interest of a man that would move the passions of others, when he feels no emotion himself; but with joy and gladness, such as angels can only know. They *sang* the story out, for they could not stop to tell it in heavy prose. They sang, "Glory to God on high, and on earth peace, good will towards men." I think they sang it with gladness in their eyes; with their hearts burning with love, and with breasts as full of joy as if the good news to man had been good news to themselves.[1]

But does the Bible state that the angels sang that night? The passage in question is found in the Gospel of Luke. On the night Christ was born, an angel appeared to some shepherds who were keeping their flocks: *Then the angel said to them, "Do not be afraid, for behold, I bring you good tidings of great joy which will be to all people. For there is born to you this day in the city of David a Savior, who is Christ the Lord. And this will be the*

sign to you: You will find a Babe wrapped in swaddling clothes, lying in a manger."

*And suddenly there was with the angel a multitude of the heavenly host **praising** God and **saying:***

"Glory to God in the highest, and on earth peace, goodwill toward men!" (Luke 2:10–14, emphisis added).

The Greek word translated as "praising" is αινουντων (*ainountōn*) from the root αινεω (*aineō*), and in a general sense, it means "to speak of the excellence of a person, object, or event."[2] More specifically, in the New Testament it is used to denote "the joyful praise of God expressed in doxology, hymn, or prayer, whether by individuals (Luke 2:20; Acts 3:8 f.), the group of disciples (Luke 19:37), the community (Acts 2:47; Revelation 19:5) or the angels (Luke 2:13)."[3]

Notice that one of the references above is Luke 2:20, which follows shortly after the announcement to the shepherds. Luke stated that when the shepherds returned from seeing the newborn Jesus, they were "glorifying and *praising* God for all the things that they had heard and seen" (emphasis added).

There is a strong connection in Scripture between singing and praising. The Psalms often instruct believers to sing their praises to God. For example, Psalm 47:6–7 states, *Sing praises to God, sing praises! Sing praises*

CHAPTER 12

The Creator in a Manger

In the beginning was the Word, and the Word was with God, and the Word was God. He was in the beginning with God. All things were made through Him, and without Him nothing was made that was made (John 1:1–3).

The Christmas classic ballet *The Nutcracker* spins the tale of a wooden nutcracker whose fight against the evil Mouse King transforms him back into a prince. The true Christmas story is far more miraculous and magnificent: the Prince of Peace took on human flesh, conquered sin and Satan by His death and Resurrection, and reconciles sinful believers to the holy God.

As the Son of God, this Prince has reigned in harmony with His Father from eternity past. The Bible begins with the truth of the Creator: *In the beginning God created the heavens and the earth* (Genesis 1:1). The Gospel of John begins similarly and identifies the agent of creation as the Son:

At Christmas time, we celebrate the day that the eternal Creator entered His creation. The Creator who stretched out the heavens was laid beneath them in a manger. The limitless Son of God took on human limitations. As a baby, Jesus depended on Joseph and Mary for care and nourishment. Yet the humility of His incarnation did not detract from the glory of His deity: *And the Word became flesh and dwelt among us, and we beheld His glory, the glory as of the only begotten of the Father, full of grace and truth* (John 1:14).

Although full of glory, the Lord Jesus was not welcomed, even from birth. The baby's cradle was a manger because no proper room could be found. Lowly shepherds visited the newborn Savior. King Herod sought to kill Jesus by ordering the slaughter of the babies in Bethlehem. Creation neither knew nor received their Creator: *He was in the world, and the world was made through Him, and*

the world did not know Him. He came to His own, and His own did not receive Him (John 1:10–11).

The same rejection happens today as "Merry Christmas" is replaced with "Happy holidays," and nativities are banned from public display. These outward changes are a sign of hearts that refuse Jesus. People hang Christmas lights yet hide their eyes from the *true Light which gives light to every man coming into the world* (John 1:9). Why? *And this is the condemnation, that the light has come into the world, and men loved darkness rather than light, because their deeds were evil. For everyone practicing evil hates the light and does not come to the light, lest his deeds should be exposed*

The Daily News

'CHRISTMAS' TREES VS. 'HOLIDAY' TREE

(John 3:19–20).

The reason so many reject Jesus, the *light of the world* (John 8:12), is because they love the sin that Christ's light exposes. Sinful mankind would rather cling to independence, immorality, idolatry, irreverence, and indulgences than turn in repentant faith to Jesus as the only Savior from sin and Lord of life.

Many continue to reject the

Prince of Peace, and the enemy, Satan, *the prince of the power of the air* (Ephesians 2:2), strives to blind men from the light: *whose minds the god of this age has blinded, who do not believe, lest the light of the gospel of the glory of Christ, who is the image of God, should shine on them* (2 Corinthians 4:4).

But there is hope. God the Father makes rescue missions

into dark enemy territory: *He has delivered us from the power of darkness and conveyed us into the kingdom of the Son of His love, in whom we have redemption through His blood, the forgiveness of sins* (Colossians 1:13–14). Redemption means to free by paying a ransom. Christ gave His life as a ransom to the Father by dying in the sinner's place (Matthew 20:28; 1 Peter 2:24).

The Son willingly gave Himself to be laid in the manger and later laid on the Cross. In his book *God's Gift of Christmas,* John MacArthur writes, "Those soft little hands, fashioned by the Holy Spirit in Mary's womb, were made so that nails might be driven through them. Those baby feet, unable to walk, would one day walk up a hill to be nailed to a cross. . . . Jesus was born to die." Yes, Jesus was born to die for sin and rise in victory.

The sinner who receives Jesus becomes a child of God: *But as many as received Him, to them He gave the right to become children of God, to those who believe in His name: who were born, not of blood, nor of the will of the flesh, nor of the will of man, but of God* (John 1:12–13). Because of Jesus' birth into this world for redemption, the sinner can be born into the family of God. That's reason to celebrate at Christmas and throughout the year!

CHAPTER 13

Why

Do We Need the

Babe

in

Bethlehem?

If Christ came to bring peace on earth and goodwill toward men (Luke 2:14), why is the earth groaning with strife and suffering?

Listening to the news reports of violence, scandals, and natural disasters makes the ringing of Christmas carols seem like childish naiveté. How could the angels have proclaimed peace on earth at the time of Christ's birth while there was so much death and destruction?

Since Adam and Eve's fall, mankind has inherited a sin-cursed world. Genesis reports how wickedness prevailed in Noah's time. The parallels between Noah's day and ours show the reality of judgment, the reach of grace, and the remedy of salvation.

JUDGMENT IS COMING!

God did not overlook the corruption in Noah's day: *Then the LORD saw that the wickedness of man was great in the earth, and that every intent of the thoughts of his heart was only evil continually* (Genesis 6:5). In judgment for sin, God promised to send a Flood to destroy man and the earth (Genesis 6:13, 17).

Most people today would agree society is also corrupt, filled with school shootings, business scandals, and crime. Yet they would blame the problem on poverty, government, or a lack of education. The average person sees himself as pretty decent. Surely on Judgment Day, God would allow such a "good" person into heaven, right? Jesus, however, said no one is good except God (Mark 10:18; Romans 3:10–12). Paul's list of serious sins, such as loving self, money, and pleasure more than God, accurately describes our world today (2 Timothy 3:1–5).

We're all born dead in our sins, following Satan to pursue selfish desires as *children of wrath* (Ephesians 2:1–3). We deserve God's wrath (Matthew 10:28; Romans 3:23, 6:23). While God promised never to send a worldwide Flood again, He is going to send a consuming fire (2 Peter 3:1–13).

"Glory to God in the highest,
And on earth peace, goodwill toward men!

—Luke 2:14

GOD GIVES GRACE If all have sinned and deserve judgment, why is anyone alive today? Not even Noah deserved to be saved from the Flood. *But Noah found grace in the eyes of the LORD* (Genesis 6:8).

Grace is an undeserved gift. We cannot earn God's saving grace by doing good works like serving in a soup kitchen, going to church, or trying to keep the Ten Commandments.

God has given everyone grace by showing Himself in creation and man's conscience (Acts 14:16–17; Romans 1:18–22, 2:14–16). Because everyone is dead in sin, sinners need the Lord's saving grace (Ephesians 2:1–10). The God of grace made one way of salvation that He revealed in His Word — the Bible.

ENTER GOD'S ONE WAY OF SALVATION. God made one way to save Noah from the Flood. Noah believed God. His faith proved genuine by his obedience in building and entering the ark (Hebrews 11:7). Still by grace through faith alone, God saves sinners today who flee His wrath against sin by turning to His one way of salvation. The Christmas account unfolds God's salvation plan.

Like Noah, Mary *found favor [grace] with God* (Luke 1:30). Like all other sinners, Mary needed God's grace. She realized this and sang praise to God her Savior (Luke 1:47).

Angels announced Jesus' birth to shepherds, calling Him *Savior, who is Christ the Lord* (Luke 2:11). These titles have

tremendous significance: *Savior* shows Jesus came to save sinners, *Christ* shows His position as the promised Messiah, and *Lord* shows His power as God in the flesh.

Jesus lived a perfect life, teaching and doing miracles that showed He was the Son of God. As the perfect sacrifice, Jesus took the punishment for sin — death — by dying on the Cross in the believer's place. He proved His victory over sin and death by rising from the dead.

God made Jesus the one way of salvation (Acts 4:12). As Noah believed God by entering the ark, sinners believe God's one way of salvation by entering into Jesus, the door of salvation (John 10:9). God saves repentant sinners from the penalty and power of sin through faith in Jesus as Savior and Lord.

Noah's salvation from the Flood through the ark pictures the believer's salvation through Jesus (1 Peter 3:18–22). Just as the waters of judgment fell on the ark instead of Noah, God's wrath against sin fell on Christ at the Cross instead of the believer (John 3:36).

Sinners must not postpone turning to Jesus. As God finally closed the door of the ark and sent the Flood, the Lord promised to again send His wrath, a surprise to people living as those in Noah's day — unprepared, unrepentant, unregenerate (Genesis 7:16–17; 2 Peter 3:1–13).

So this Christmas, remember that peace on earth comes only through Jesus. His sacrifice on the Cross made peace between God and believing sinners (Colossians 1:20; Romans 5:1). One day, after judgment, His peace will reign forever. Enter into Jesus, the ark of salvation!

I am the door. If anyone enters by Me, he will be saved, and will go in and out and find pasture.

— John 10:9

CHAPTER 14

What is the Significance of the Name "JESUS"?

THE NAME JESUS Why did the angel tell Mary and Joseph to name the baby "Jesus"? Is there some holy significance to this particular sequence of letters or sounds? No, these letters and sounds are different in every language into which the name of Jesus is translated. The name of Jesus is not *phonologically* unique; it was a fairly common Jewish name and is still used today, though not in English. For example, Jesús is a fairly common name in many Hispanic countries.

"Jesus" is an English rendering of the Greek name *Iēsous*, which is a translation of the ancient Hebrew *Yehoshua*. This name is formed from Hebrew roots signifying "Jehovah is salvation" and is translated in our English Old Testament as "Joshua." The Greek version of this name also refers to Joshua once in the New Testament (Hebrews 4:8).

The name of Jesus is significant because of who it represents — it means "God our Savior." Jesus Christ is *Immanuel,* "God with us" (Matthew 1:23). He came to earth as a man in order to die in our place and become our Savior. This is why the angel said, *You shall call His name JESUS, for He will save His people from their sins* (Matthew 1:21).

The name of Jesus reminds us about the amazing humility of the Son of God when He came as a man to die. As His followers, we must strive to show the same selfless humility that Jesus demonstrated while on earth:

Let this mind be in you which was also in Christ Jesus, who, being in the form of God, did not consider it robbery to be equal with God, but made Himself of no reputation, taking the form of a bondservant, and coming in the likeness of men. And being found in appearance as a man, He humbled Himself and became obedient to the point of death, even the death of the cross (Philippians 2:5–8).

However, Jesus is not just a name of unmatched humility; it is also a name of infinite

God
Jesus
Christ
King of Kings
Gift of God
Alpha & Omega
The Lamb of God
Redeemer, Deliverer
Glory of Israel, Bread of Life
Anointed of God, Beloved of God
Son of God, Word, Teacher of God
Son of Man, Eternal Life, Word of Life
Root of Jesse, Servant, Witness, Holy One
Mediator, Advocate, Passover, Shepherd, Master
Image of God, Prophet, Truth, Way, Redeemer
Jehovah, Nazarene, Messiah, Ruler, Son of David
Lord of Hosts, Messenger of the Covenant, Truth, Judge
Wonderful, Counselor, Mighty God, Everlasting, Prince of Peace
Friend of Sinners, Finisher of Faith
Emmanuel

exaltation. His name is glorified far above every other name: *Therefore God also has highly exalted Him and given Him the name which is above every name, that at the name of Jesus every knee should bow, of those in heaven, and of those on earth, and of those under the earth, and that every tongue should confess that Jesus Christ is Lord, to the glory of God the Father* (Philippians 2:9–11; cf. Acts 4:12).

WHY ARE THE GENEALOGIES OF CHRIST IMPORTANT? In

our modern culture — especially in America — many families have little sense of heritage. We may have some family traditions, but most Americans don't even know the names of their great, great grandparents or care where they lived or what they did, etc. Modern genealogy is primarily reserved for hobbyists. In contrast, genealogies were a deeply integral part of Jewish society at the time of Jesus. Land was inherited based on family lines, and those who could not prove their ancestry in Israel were considered outsiders.

Because of this difference, modern readers usually skip right over the genealogies in Scripture. The "begats" may not be fascinating reading, but don't disregard them. God had reasons for inspiring every part of the Bible — even the genealogies of Christ.

Imagine accurately tracing your ancestry back 4,000 years. As incredible as it sounds, the biblical lineage of Jesus does just that. His genealogy is recorded all the way back to the first man, Adam. This is not an insignificant detail; it is a crucial fulfillment of prophecy. Adam's sin brought judgment and death into the world, but a Savior was promised — the Seed of the woman who would strike the head of the serpent (Genesis 3:15). Jesus Christ is the "Last Adam" (1 Corinthians 15:45), the promised Seed of the woman, which Paul summarized: *Therefore, as through one man's offense judgment came to all men, resulting in condemnation, even so through one Man's righteous act the free gift came to all men, resulting in justification of life* (Romans 5:18).

Jesus is the Savior who was promised throughout history.

The genealogies in Matthew and Luke show Him as the descendant of Abraham, Isaac, Jacob, and eventually David — men to whom these prophecies were made. God promised Abraham that all nations would be blessed through his offspring, which was ultimately fulfilled in Jesus Christ (Galatians 3:7–9, 16).

By reading these genealogies, we see that Jesus was a direct descendant of King David. This is also a fulfillment of many Old Testament promises, which today's passage demonstrates. The promised Messiah would be the descendant of David (2 Samuel 7:12–14) and would one day rule on David's throne (Isaiah 9:6–7).

Jesus Christ has fulfilled these and will eventually fulfill every

Now Jesus Himself began His ministry at about thirty years of age, being (as was supposed) the son of Joseph, the son of Heli, the son of Matthat, the son of Levi, the son of Melchi, the son of Janna, the son of Joseph, the son of Mattathiah, the son of Amos, the son of Nahum, the son of Esli, the son of Naggai, the son of Maath, the son of Mattathiah, the son of Semei, the son of Joseph, the son of Judah, the son of Joannas, the son of Rhesa, the son of Zerubbabel, the son of Shealtiel, the son of Neri, the son of Melchi, the son of Addi, the son of Cosam, the son of Elmodam, the son of Er, the son of Jose, the son of Eliezer, the son of Jorim, the son of Matthat, the son of Levi, the son of Simeon, the son of Judah, the son of Joseph, the son of Jonan, the son of Eliakim, the son of Melea, the son of Menan, the son of Mattathah, the son of Nathan, the son of David, the son of Jesse, the son of Obed, the son of Boaz, the son of Salmon, the son of Nahshon, the son of Amminadab, the son of Ram, the son of Hezron, the son of Perez, the son of Judah, the son of Jacob, the son of Isaac, the son of Abraham, the son of Terah, the son of Nahor, the son of Serug, the son of Reu, the son of Peleg, the son of Eber, the son of Shelah, the son of Cainan, the son of Arphaxad, the son of Shem, the son of Noah, the son of Lamech, the son of Methuselah, the son of Enoch, the son of Jared, the son of Mahalalel, the son of Cainan, the son of Enosh, the son of Seth, the son of Adam, the son of God.

Luke 3:23-38

messianic prophecy in Scripture. He is the promised Messiah — the descendant of Abraham and David — our Savior who gave His life to redeem us from our sins.

How Christmas

Happy Holidays!

Came To Be

CHAPTER 15

What was the Christmas Star?

The Apostle Matthew records that the birth of Jesus was accompanied by an extraordinary celestial event: a star that led the magi[1] (the "wise men") to Jesus. This star *went before them, till it came and stood over where the young Child was* (Matthew 2:9). What was this star? How did it lead the magi to the Lord? There have been many speculations.

COMMON EXPLANATIONS

The star mentioned in Matthew is not necessarily what we normally think of as a star. That is, it was not necessarily an enormous mass of hydrogen and helium gas powered by nuclear fusion. The Greek word translated *star* is *aster (αστηρ)*, which is where we get the word *astronomy*. In the biblical conception of the word, a star is any luminous point of light in our night sky. This would certainly include our modern definition of a star, but it would also include the planets, supernovae, comets, or anything else that resembles a point of light. But which of these explanations best describes the Christmas star?

A supernova (an exploding star) fits the popular Christmas card conception of the star. When a star in our galaxy explodes, it shines very brightly for several months. These beautiful events are quite rare and outshine all the other stars in the galaxy. It seems fitting that such a spectacular event would announce the birth of the King of kings — the God-man who would outshine all others. However, a supernova does not fit the biblical text. The Christmas star must not have been so obvious, for it went unnoticed by Israel's King Herod (Matthew 2:7). He had to ask the magi when the star had appeared, but everyone would have seen a bright supernova.

Nor could the Christmas star have been a bright comet. Like a supernova, everyone would have noticed a comet. Comets were often considered to be omens of change in the ancient

Some have thought the Christmas Star might have been a supernova, like the one seen here in M83, a spiral galaxy.

world. Herod would not have needed to ask the magi when a comet had appeared. Moreover, neither a comet nor a supernova moves in such a way as to come and stand over a location on earth as the Christmas star did (Matthew 2:9). Perhaps the Christmas star was something more subtle: a sign that would amaze the magi but would not be noticed by Herod.

A CONJUNCTION? This leads us to the theory that the Christmas star was a *conjunction* of planets. A conjunction is when a planet passes closely by a star or by another planet. Such an event would have been very meaningful to the magi, who were knowledgeable of ancient astronomy, but would likely have gone unnoticed by others. There were several interesting conjunctions around the time of Christ's birth. Two of these were triple conjunctions; this is when a planet passes a star (or another planet), then backs up, passes it again, then reverses direction and passes the star/planet a third time. Such events are quite rare.

Nonetheless, there was a triple conjunction of Jupiter and Saturn beginning in the year 7 B.C. Also, there was a triple conjunction of Jupiter and the bright star Regulus beginning in the year 3 B.C. Of course, we do not know the exact year of Christ's birth, but both of these events are close to the estimated time. Advocates of such conjunction theories point out that the

The heavens declare the glory of God;
And the firmament shows
His handiwork.

— Psalm 19:1

planets and stars involved had important religious significance in the ancient world. Jupiter was often considered the king of the gods, and Regulus was considered the "king star." Did such a conjunction announce the birth of the King of kings? However, the Bible describes the Christmas star as a single star — not a conjunction of two or more stars. Neither of the above conjunctions was close enough to appear as a single star.

But there was one (and *only* one) extraordinary conjunction around the time of Christ's birth that could be called a "star." In the year 2 B.C., Jupiter and Venus moved so close to each other that they briefly appeared to merge into a single bright star. Such an event is extremely rare and may have been perceived as highly significant to the magi. Although this event would have been really spectacular, it does not fully match the description of the Christmas star. A careful reading of the biblical text indicates that the magi saw the star on at least two occasions: when they arrived at Jerusalem (Matthew 2:2) and after meeting with Herod (Matthew 2:9). But the merging of Jupiter and Venus happened only once — on the evening of June 17.

Although each of the above events is truly spectacular and may have been fitting to announce the birth of the King of kings, none of them seems to fully satisfy the details of the straightforward reading of Matthew 2. None of the above

speculations fully explain how the star *went ahead of* the magi nor how it *stood over where the child was*. Indeed, no known natural phenomenon would be able to stand over Bethlehem since all natural stars continually move due to the rotation of the earth.[2] They appear to rise in the east and set in the west, or circle around the celestial poles. However, the Bible does not say that this star was a natural phenomenon.

NATURAL LAW Of course, God can use natural law to accomplish His will. In fact, the laws of nature are really just descriptions of the way that God normally upholds the universe and accomplishes His will. But God is not bound by natural law; He is free to act in other ways if He so chooses. The Bible records a number of occasions where God acted in a seemingly unusual way to accomplish an extraordinary purpose.

The virgin birth itself was a supernatural event; it cannot be explained within the context of known natural laws. For that matter, God previously used apparently supernatural signs in the heavens as a guide. In Exodus 13:21, we find that God guided the Israelites with a cloud by day and a pillar of fire by night. It should not be surprising that a supernatural sign in the heavens would accompany the birth of the Son of God. The star that led the magi seems to be one of those incredible acts of God — specially de-signed and created for a unique purpose.[3] Let us examine what this star did according to Matthew 2.

PURPOSE OF THE STAR

First, the star alerted the magi to the birth of Christ, prompting them to make the long trek to Jerusalem. These magi were *"from the East"* according to verse 1; they are generally thought to be from Persia, which is east of Jerusalem. If so, they may have had some knowledge of the Scriptures since the prophet Daniel had also lived in that region centuries earlier. Perhaps the magi were expecting a new star to announce the birth of Christ from reading Numbers 24:17, which describes a star coming

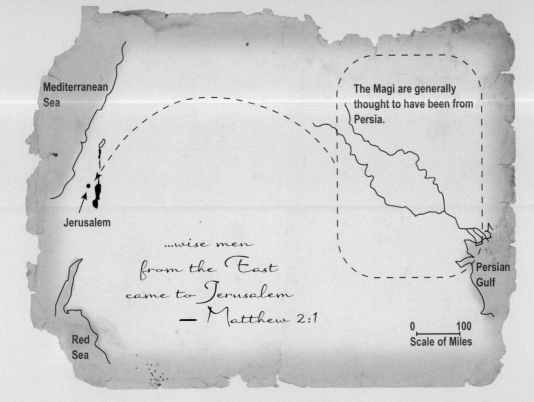

Mediterranean Sea

The Magi are generally thought to have been from Persia.

Jerusalem

...wise men from the East came to Jerusalem
— Matthew 2:1

Persian Gulf

Red Sea

0   100
Scale of Miles

from Jacob and a King ("*Scepter*")[4] from Israel.[5]

Curiously, the magi seem to have been the only ones who saw the star — or at least the only ones who understood its meaning. Recall that King Herod had to ask the magi when the star had appeared (Matthew 2:7). If the magi alone saw the star, this further supports the notion that the Christmas star was a supernatural manifestation from God rather than a common star, which would

have been visible to all. The fact that the magi referred to it as "*His star*" further supports the unique nature of the star.[6]

The position of the star when the magi first saw it is disputed. The Bible says that they "saw His star in the east" (Matthew 2:2). Does this mean that the *star* was in the eastward heavens when they first saw it, or does it mean that the *magi* were "in the East" (i.e., Persia) when they saw the star?[7] If the star was in the east, why did the magi travel

west? Recall that the Bible does not say that the star guided the magi to Jerusalem (though it may have); we only know for certain that it went before them on the journey from Jerusalem to the house of Christ. It is possible that the star initially acted only as a sign, rather than as a guide. The magi may have headed to Jerusalem only because this would have seemed a logical place to begin their search for the King of the Jews.

But there is another interesting possibility. The Greek phrase translated *in the east (εν ανατολη)* can also be translated *at its rising*. The expression can be used to refer to the east since all normal stars rise in the east (due to earth's rotation). But the Christmas star may have been a supernatural exception — rising in the *west* over Bethlehem (which from the distance of Persia would have been indistinguishable from Jerusalem). The wise men would have recognized such a unique rising. Perhaps they took it as a sign that the prophecy of Numbers 24:17 was fulfilled since the star quite literally rose from Israel.

CLEARING UP MISCONCEPTIONS

Contrary to what is commonly believed, the magi did not arrive at the manger on the night of Christ's birth; rather, they found the young Jesus and His mother living in a house (Matthew 2:11). This could have been nearly two years after Christ's birth (see chapter 6), since Herod — afraid that his own position as king was threatened — tried to have Jesus eliminated by killing all male children under the age of two (Matthew 2:16).

It seems that the star was not visible at the time the magi reached Jerusalem but then reappeared when they began their (much shorter) journey from Jerusalem to the Bethlehem region, approximately 6 miles (10 km) away. This view is supported by the fact that first, the magi had to ask King Herod where the King of the Jews was born, which means the star wasn't guiding them at that time (Matthew 2:2). And second, they rejoiced exceedingly when they saw the star (again) as they began their journey to Bethlehem (Matthew 2:10).

After the magi had met with Herod, the star went on before them to the Bethlehem region[8] and stood over the location of Jesus. It seems to have led them to the very house that Jesus was in — not just the city. The magi already knew that Christ was in the Bethlehem region. This they had learned from Herod, who had learned it from the priests and scribes (Matthew 2:4–5, 8). For a normal star, it would be impossible to determine which house is directly beneath it. The star over Christ may have been relatively near the surface of earth (an "atmospheric" manifestation of God's power) so that the magi could discern the precise location of the Child.

Whatever the exact mechanism, the fact that the star led the magi to Christ is evidence that God uniquely designed the star for a very special purpose. God can use extraordinary means for extraordinary purposes. Certainly the birth of our Lord was deserving of honor in the heavens. It is fitting that God used a celestial object to announce the birth of Christ since *The heavens declare the glory of God*" (Psalm 19:1).

(Endnotes)

1   Magi (pronounced ma'ji') were scholars of the ancient world, possibly a class of Zoroastrian priests from Media or Persia. It is commonly assumed that three magi came on the journey to visit Christ since they brought three gifts. However, the Bible does not actually give the number of magi.

2   The star that moves the least is the North Star because it is almost directly in line with the earth's North Pole. However, this would not have been the case at the time of Christ's birth, due to a celestial phenomenon called "precession." There was no "North Star" during Christ's earthly ministry.

3   Although this star seems to break all the rules, it is perhaps even more amazing that essentially all the other stars do not. The fact that all the stars in our night sky obey orderly logical laws of nature is consistent with biblical creation and inconsistent with secular notions. For more information on the laws of nature, see www.answersingenesis.org/articles/am/v1/n2/god-natural-law.

4   This verse makes use of synecdoche — the part represents the whole. In this case, the scepter represents a scepter bearer (i.e., a king). This is clear from the synonymous parallelism (see the next note).

5   This verse is written in synonymous parallelism, which is a form of Hebrew poetry in which a statement is made followed by a very similar statement with the same basic meaning. "A star shall come forth from Jacob, and a Scepter shall rise from Israel." Both statements poetically indicate the coming of a future king (Christ). Star and Scepter (bearer) both indicate a king, and Israel and Jacob are two names for the same person who is the ancestor of the coming king.

6   Granted, all stars were created by God and therefore belong to Him. But the Christmas star is specially designated as "His" (Christ's), suggesting its unusual nature.

7   The latter view is indicated by John Gill in his commentary.

8   Although we know Christ was born in the town of Bethlehem, there is no reason to suppose that He remained there for the entire time of the magi's journey. We know that Christ's family brought Him to the temple in Jerusalem after the days of purification (Luke 2:22); it is possible that they went directly to Nazareth after that (Luke 2:39) and then returned to Bethlehem sometime later. The wise men apparently did meet Christ in the Bethlehem region, however. We know this because as soon as they departed, God warned Joseph (Matthew 2:13) that Herod was about to kill all the male children in Bethlehem and its environs (Matthew 2:16), necessitating the escape to Egypt.

CHAPTER 16

The Virgin Birth

With the sale of over 80 million copies of *The Da Vinci Code* book and a blockbuster film, the question is constantly raised: Is Jesus Christ really the Son of God, or was He just another human, but a better one?

The deity of Jesus (the assertion that He is both God and man) is so vital to the gospel that, if not true, there is no hope for salvation. If Jesus' deity were not true, it would take the good news out of the gospel and make the story of Jesus a greeting card, and nothing more.

The virgin birth is a miracle. The Bible gives no details, scientifically, of how God did it. But what He does tell us is that it was by the power of the Holy Spirit. God came over a human womb, and a child was conceived — a child who was 100 percent man and 100 percent God, with a human mother and God as His father.

This miracle, in terms of apologetics, falls back on the attributes and power of the Father. Let's consider these rhetorical questions:

1. Did God create the universe?

2. Since He created and designed the universe and its systems, is He above the scientific laws He set in motion?

3. Because He is above those laws, when He did become man, were His actions, lifestyle, and testimony unlike any other?

4. His lifestyle, His ministry, His rejection by sinful men — do these all give credibility to the claim that Jesus came from God the Father?

5. Does His Resurrection from the grave also verify His claims of being the Son of God?

6. Has man sinned?

The answer to all these questions is, of course, "Yes!" Romans 3:23 tells us we need a Savior. So God sent His Son in this miraculous way. Jesus was both God and man. He was

God, so He was sinless; and yet He was man, so He could take our place. If you reject the truth of the virgin birth, you redefine Jesus as just a man. Do that and you remain in your condemned state before God, for only the blood of the incarnate Christ can cleanse you of sin (Hebrews 9:12). If you acknowledge this truth, believe on and place your trust in Jesus as the resurrected Son of God, you will be saved and have eternal life (John 10:27–28).

CHAPTER 17

Did Mary remain a Virgin?

Mary, the mother of Jesus, was an incredible woman. In fact, precious few women's names could even be mentioned to give her a "run for her money." In fact, God honored Mary in a way that all other women could only dream about. The Lord favored her for an event that had been long-awaited since the Genesis 3:15 prophecy of the Seed of a woman (i.e., the virgin birth): *And having come in, the angel said to her, "Rejoice, highly favored one, the Lord is with you; blessed are you among women!"*

But when she saw him, she was troubled at his saying, and considered what manner of greeting this was. Then the angel said to her, "Do not be afraid, Mary, for you have found favor with God.

And behold, you will conceive in your womb and bring forth a Son, and shall call His name JESUS. He will be great, and will be called the Son of the Highest; and the Lord God will give Him the throne of His father David. And He will reign over the house of Jacob forever, and of His kingdom there will be no end."

Then Mary said to the angel, "How can this be, since I do not know a man?"

And the angel answered and said to her, "The Holy Spirit will come upon you, and the power of the Highest will overshadow you; therefore, also, that Holy One who is to be born will be called the Son of God" (Luke 1:28–35).

Mary was a virgin who was to conceive by being overshadowed by the Holy Spirit and giving birth to the Son of God. Few in Christian realms would deny Mary was a virgin and remained a virgin through pregnancy and the birth of Christ. This was the ultimate fulfillment of a prophecy from Isaiah:

*Therefore the Lord Himself will give you a sign: Behold, **the virgin shall conceive and bear a Son,** and shall call His name Immanuel* (Isaiah 7:14, emphasis added).

Following is a table of some contradictions between *The Protoevangelium of James* and the Bible:

PROTOEVANGELIUM OF JAMES[4]	THE BIBLE
1. Gabriel is called an archangel (chapter 9:22), which was a common designation for Gabriel in apocryphal literature written after the first century. (For example, see *Revelation of Paul, The Book of John Concerning the Falling Asleep of Mary,* and *The Apocalypse of the Holy Mother of God.*)	The Bible never identifies Gabriel as an archangel, but Michael is described as an archangel in Jude 1:9. The idea of Gabriel as an archangel seems to be a misconception that began in the second century.
2. Mary's response to the angel is different than what is recorded in Scripture. "What! Shall I conceive by the living God, and bring forth as all other women do?" (chapter 9:12).[5]	Luke 1:34 states, *Then Mary said to the angel, 'How can this be, since I do not know a man?'*
3. Elizabeth fled the Bethlehem region with her son John (the Baptist) to the mountains because of Herod's wrath when he decided to kill all the baby boys around and in Bethlehem (chapter 16:3).	Concerning John the Baptist, Luke 1:80 states, *So the child grew and became strong in spirit, and was in the deserts till the day of his manifestation to Israel.* It was Joseph, Mary, and Jesus who fled from Bethlehem because of Herod (Matthew 2:13–15).
4. Jesus was born in a cave outside the city of Bethlehem (chapters 12:11–14:31).	Jesus was born in Bethlehem, the town of David, according to Luke 2:4, 11 and Matthew 2:1.

PROTOEVANGELIUM OF JAMES[4]	THE BIBLE
5 The angel of the Lord, when speaking to Joseph in a dream, said to take Mary but does not mention having her as a wife. The priest chastised Joseph and accused him for taking Mary as a wife secretly by the priest. Joseph takes her home but is reluctant to call her his wife when they go to Bethlehem (Chapters 10:17–18, 11:14, 12:2–3).	Matthew 1:19 reveals that Joseph was already Mary's husband (they were betrothed) before the angel visited him in a dream. Matthew 1:24 points out that after the angel visited Joseph, he kept her as his wife.
6 Mary wrapped Jesus in swaddling cloths and hid him in a manger at the inn to keep him from the massacre by Herod's men (chapter 16:2).	Mary and Joseph were warned of Herod's plot by an angel, and they fled to Egypt (Matthew 2:13–14).
7 Wise men came to Bethlehem and inquired of Herod where the Child was born (chapter 21:1–2).	Wise men came to Jerusalem to inquire where the child king was (Matthew 2:1).

The Codex Tchacos contained the first known copy of the Gospel of Judas, an early work reportedly rejected by the Church as heresy. Much of its history, origin and even meaning are still being studied today by historians and theologians.

CONCLUSION *The Protoevangelium of James* contains the first known mention of Mary's continual virginity. Likely, this book influenced subsequent people to write of the perpetual virginity of Mary. But the book was not the work of the Apostle James, the brother of Christ. The work's demotion by the early Church, especially its non-inclusion with other books of the canon due to its numerous errors, is further verification it was not authentic.

Keep in mind that no passage of Scripture states Mary perpetually remained a virgin and many state the opposite. So to make a case for the perpetual virginity of Mary, one must use ideas that come from outside the Bible and then reinterpret Scripture with some wild hermeneutical gymnastics. This would be appealing to fallible, sinful ideas that originate in the minds of mankind — not God. Why not trust God when He speaks? After all, it would not be a sin for Mary to have sexual relations with her husband Joseph, but it would have been sinful for her to withhold herself from him throughout their marriage (1 Corinthians 7:3–5). There is no biblical or logical reason why Mary would have needed to remain a virgin following the birth of Christ.

The issue is quite simple: should we trust the imperfect sources and traditions that come from outside of Scripture and contradict it or should we trust God's Word?

(Endnotes)

1   Some have suggested that Joseph may have died before fathering children with Mary so that these sons and daughters were the children of Mary and another husband. However, it seems unlikely that Jesus would have been called "the carpenter's son" if His earthly father had died some 20–30 years earlier. Furthermore, even the people in Capernaum (roughly 20 miles from Nazareth) recognized Him as "the son of Joseph" and claimed to "know" (present tense) His father and mother (John 6:42). Although the Bible does not record Joseph's death, it likely happened prior to the Lord's Crucifixion since Jesus entrusted John with the care of His mother (John 19:27).

2   Adam Clarke, *Clarke's Commentary*, electronic edition (New York: Carlton & Phillips, 1853), Matthew 13:55.

3   Origen's Commentary on Matthew in Ante-Nicene Fathers Volume IX. http://www.ccel.org/ccel/schaff/anf09.xvi.ii.iii.xvii.html.

4   Quotations are from *The Protoevangelium of James*, translated by Alexander Walker, Esq., in Alexander Roberts and James Donaldson, *The Ante-Nicene Fathers*, electronic ed. (Garland, TX: Galaxie Software, 2000).

5   Another translation of this work is available at http://ministries.tliquest.net/theology/apocryphas/nt/protevan.htm. Mary's reply is rendered differently in this version, in which she replied, "What! By the living God, shall I conceive and bring forth as all other women do?" The angel responded, "Not so, O Mary, but the Holy Spirit will come upon you, and the power of the Most High will overshadow you." This version makes better sense, since the angel corrects her thinking that this would occur via natural means. Walker's translation (cited in the table) makes little sense. Mary assumes it would be a supernatural conception, and then the angel "corrects" her by telling her it would be supernatural. However, both versions of The Protoevangelium of James have Mary knowing more at this point than she does in the biblical account. In the Bible, Mary wonders how she could become pregnant since she was a virgin. In *The Protoevangelium of James*, she seems to guess right away that this would be a supernatural event.

CHAPTER 18

Mary Did You Know?

DID MARY KNOW? *"And behold, you will conceive in your womb and bring forth a Son, and shall call His name* JESUS. *He will be great, and will be called the Son of the Highest; and the Lord God will give Him the throne of His father David. And He will reign over the house of Jacob forever, and of His kingdom there will be no end"* (Luke 1:31–33).

An angel came to Mary and told her about the birth of the Messiah. A prophecy of the coming of Jesus and what He came to do was nothing new, as there are many such statements in the Old Testament. However, we can now more easily recognize those prophecies and what they mean since we have the New Testament. Today's question has been brought up before in the form of a Christmas song, which is entitled, *"Mary, Did You Know?"*

Ironically, after the angel told Mary of her Son and that He is the Son of the Lord God, she asked, *"How can this be, since I do not know a man?"* (Luke 1:34). This could make one wonder if she truly understood the angel's words. Of course, having an angel appear to you did not happen everyday (even in biblical times), let alone having one proclaim that you will give birth to the Son of God.

Mary wondered how this could come about physically, yet this is no reason to find fault with her. There is no indication that she actually doubted, though she was definitely curious. We must remember that this was not the first time that someone wondered about how a prophecy would come about (e.g., Abraham and Sarah or Zacharias). If we were in their shoes, we might have done the same thing.

The angel described that the Holy Spirit would accomplish these things. After that, Mary acknowledged her trust in the Lord that it would come to pass and her willing obedience to the plan.

Scripture never specifically states that Mary realized that

her Son was to die on the Cross, but Mary did state the following: "*My soul magnifies the Lord, and my spirit has rejoiced in God my Savior. For He has regarded the lowly state of His maidservant; for behold, henceforth all generations will call me blessed*" (Luke 1:46–48).

Mary realized that her Son was the Son of God, and that He would affect the generations to come. Furthermore, with all the things that happened to Mary, how could she not realize that there was something special about this baby? Mary is a good example of how we should also trust in the Lord's promises that He has given to us through His Word — whether we completely understand all the details or not.

But we speak the wisdom of God in a mystery, the hidden wisdom which God ordained before the ages for our glory, which none of the rulers of this age knew; for had they known, they would not have crucified the Lord of glory (1 Corinthians 2:7–8).

DID OTHERS KNOW WHAT WAS TO COME?

Previously, we discussed whether Mary knew what was to come for baby Jesus. There are many prophecies in the Old Testament foretelling the coming Messiah and the sacrifice He would make (Isaiah 53:8; Daniel 9:26). Here, we will study whether people recognized these prophecies and associated them with Jesus.

Scripture is clear that "*none of the rulers of this age knew.*" In fact, if they did realize, "*they would not have crucified the Lord of glory.*" Jesus actually talked about His death and Resurrection during His earthly ministry: "*Destroy this temple, and in three days I will raise it up*" (John 2:19; cf. Matthew 20:17–18). Yet people still did not understand His words, as they thought He referred to the physical temple (John 2:20–22).

When Jesus arrived in Jerusalem, there was a big crowd of people shouting, "*Hosanna! 'Blessed is He who comes in the name of the* Lord*!' The King of Israel!*" (John 12:13). They expected Him to be their earthly king, but that was not the purpose of His coming. Many of these same people likely shouted for His crucifixion when Jesus was on trial a few days later.

Not even the disciples completely understood everything that was said and done until Jesus was glorified (John 12:16), although Jesus was preparing them for their future ministries. He said that the Holy Spirit would be sent to them so that they would recall all that was said after everything was accomplished (John 14:26).

The shepherds recognized that there was something special about Jesus when they saw Him that day, as they were *glorifying and praising God for all the things that they had heard and seen, as it was told them* (Luke 2:20). They likely did not fully understand what was to come, but they took the angels at their word and spread the good news about Christ Jesus the Messiah.

Moreover, Simeon understood that Jesus was destined to affect many hearts and also indicated to Mary that her Son would suffer (Luke 2:34–35). No details were given, so it is hard to know whether Simeon or Mary fully understood what that meant.

God knew what He was doing all along; before Jesus was born, He knew people would not understand. There was a reason God's wisdom remained hidden: God's plan for Jesus Christ needed to come to pass before this mystery was to be revealed to everyone.

CHAPTER 19

Uncovering
the
Real
Nativity

CHRISTMAS TRADITION

Christmas is a favorite time of the year for many of us. It's a season full of joyful celebration and family traditions. It's a time of hustle and bustle and last-minute shopping in search of the ideal gift. The average home might be adorned inside and out with swags of evergreen garland and large wreaths tied with velvety red bows.

Inside, a toasty fire crackles beneath a row of overfilled stockings, and the air is filled with the wafting scent of cinnamon and apple cider. And in some homes, somewhere under the Christmas tree, beneath twinkling lights and billowing tinsel, nestled behind mountains of brightly wrapped boxes and bows, you might find a little nativity set.

It's a familiar scene. The average nativity shows Mary and Joseph positioned in the center of the rustic setting, surrounded by cattle, sheep, and donkeys — all facing the newborn king. The shepherds stand over to one side . . . all lined up in a semi-circular row. Across from them are three wisemen with their gifts of gold, frankincense, and myrrh. All this takes place in a stable. After all, the Bible says Mary laid the baby Jesus in a manger, and mangers are found in barns and stables, right? In fact, didn't we read that the innkeeper had no room for them in the inn, so he reluctantly let them stay out back in his stable?

But wait . . . does the Bible really fill in all these details? Or have we added tradition upon tradition until the glittery scene before us hardly resembles the real historical event — the night of our Savior's birth.

ARCHAEOLOGY AND THE BIBLE

During His earthly ministry, Jesus said that if His followers would neglect to praise Him, the very *stones would . . . cry out* (Luke 19:40). And that's exactly what they've done.

The science of archaeology was born in the early 19th century, not all that long ago. Many wondered if this emerging science would support the biblical account as real history, or reveal the text to be nothing more than wishful thinking, an elaborate fairy tale, or a diabolical hoax. However, since that time,

more than 25,000 biblical sites have been discovered. Scripture has been confirmed by archaeology in tens of thousands of details. In fact, even when archaeologists were sure they would find something to discredit some portion of Scripture they only ended up doing the opposite.

So what does the Bible and archaeology have to say about the birth of Jesus? As it turns out, plenty. Before we begin, quiz yourself to see if you can separate biblical truth from holiday tradition: True or False?

1. Mary was in labor when she got into town, so Joseph had to take whatever lodging he could get.

2. The Bible uses the Greek word kataluma — translated "inn." Kataluma means "small hotel."

3. The Bible says that Mary and Joseph spent the night in a stable.

4. The innkeeper told Mary and Joseph there was no room for them in the inn.

5. The innkeeper's wife brought water and towels

to Mary and assisted in Jesus' birth.

6. The Bible says there were three wise men.

7. The wise men were present the night of Christ's birth.

Believe it or not, all of these statements are false. (See end of this chapter for explanation.)

BACK TO THE BIBLE Most people think of Answers in Genesis as a creation vs. evolution ministry, but our purpose and mission is to uphold the authority of Scripture.

God's Word is the final authority on all matters about which it speaks — not just the moral and spiritual matters, but also its teachings that bear on history and archaeology — indeed all sciences. Therefore, the Bible informs and guides our interpretation of archaeology and, at the same time, archaeology bolsters our faith in the accuracy and infallibility of God's Word.

For centuries, the traditional "Christmas story" has been told and retold many times in books, sermons, plays, and movies — so much so that the line between tradition and biblical reality is often blurred to the point that our minds tend to fill in details that aren't really in the biblical text.

For example, this may surprise you, but the Bible actually makes no mention of an innkeeper in Bethlehem. There probably wasn't really an inn the way we think of an inn — like a little hotel, of sorts. Mary and Joseph might not have stayed in a stable — at least not the way we think of a stable. And not only do we suspect that there were not three wise men, they probably weren't present the night Jesus was born.

In 1 Thessalonians 5:21, we are instructed to *Test all things, hold fast what is good.* For this reason, then, we are investigating and rethinking some of the holiday traditions that have been assigned to the biblical text.

We want to be like the Berean Christians who *received the word with all readiness, and searched the scriptures daily, whether those things were so* (Acts 17:11). Our goal is not to attack long-held traditions, but to gently set them aside for the sake of the truth and get back to what the Bible really says.

NO ROOM IN THE INN Let's take a look at the account of Christ's birth as written in the Gospel of Luke: *And it came to pass in those days that a decree went out from Caesar Augustus that all the world should be registered. . . . So all went to be registered, everyone to his own city.*

Joseph also went up from Galilee, out of the city of Nazareth, into Judea, to the city of David, which is called Bethlehem, because he was of the house and lineage of David, to be registered with Mary, his betrothed wife, who was with child. So it was, that while they were there, the *days were completed for her to be delivered. And she brought forth her firstborn Son, and wrapped Him in swaddling cloths, and laid Him in a manger, because there was no room for them in the inn* (Luke 2:1–7).

Already we have an image in our minds based on traditions that we grew up with. It might go something like this: Joseph gets into town late and there's a "no vacancy" sign hanging outside the little inn. He desperately pounds on the door and pleads with the innkeeper, who eventually takes pity on the weary couple and sends them around back to the stable. The innkeeper's compassionate wife quickly scrounges around for some clean water and blankets . . . and just in time, too, because Mary is already in labor.

But wait. Does the Bible actually say that? Lets take a closer look at the text. In verses 3 and 4 we see that Joseph is traveling to the home of his family.

So all went to be registered, everyone to his own city.

Joseph also went up from Galilee, out of the city of Nazareth, into Judea, to the city of David, which is called Bethlehem, because he was of the house and lineage of David.

In the Hebrew culture, it would have been customary for Joseph to stay in the home of his rela-

And she brought forth her firstborn Son, and wrapped Him in swaddling cloths, and laid Him in a manger, because there was no room for them in the inn.

— Luke 2:7

tives, in the guest room, not in a local inn. Some might argue that Joseph probably headed to an inn rather than to his family because he was afraid he might be shunned, considering Mary's condition outside of wedlock. But there is more to this picture than meets the eye.

Did Mary give birth the night they arrived in Bethlehem? Well, verse 6 says: *So it was, that while they were there, the days were completed for her to be delivered.*

This text seems to indicate that they were there for a while before Mary gave birth. If Joseph could find nothing more than a stable that first night, it seems he could have found something better before Mary had her baby. Verse 7 says: *And she*

brought forth her firstborn Son, and wrapped Him in swaddling cloths, and laid Him in a manger, because there was no room for them in the inn.

"Inn." Doesn't that refer to a hotel, or something like one? Actually, the Greek word translated here as "inn" is the word kataluma, which usually refers to a "guest room." The word kataluma only occurs two other times in Scripture — both of those are translated "guest room," and they refer to the upper room where Jesus gave instructions to His disciples regarding the Last Supper: *"Where is the guest room [the kataluma] in which I may eat the Passover with My disciples?"* (Mark 14:14; see also Luke 22:11).

You may recall that Luke does refer to an "inn" and an "innkeeper" in the parable of the Good Samaritan, but there, instead of the word kataluma, Luke uses the word pandocheion which means "an inn, a public house for the reception of strangers." So when you read "inn," think "guest room." Now that certainly paints a different picture, doesn't it? She laid Him in a manger, because there was no room for them in the guest room.

THE GUEST ROOM (KATALUMA) We'll probably never be able to dig up first-century Bethlehem. It's been built over many times and is considered a holy site by some groups since it is the town of King David and the birthplace of our Lord. But

archaeologists have recently uncovered and reconstructed other first-century towns that are probably very similar to the Bethlehem of Jesus' day.

These reconstructions give us a better picture of the homes that occupied the hillsides of Judea at the time of Jesus' birth. Some of these homes were multiple stories tall, and some were only one. A multiple-story home was often built into the side of a hill. The lower portion of the house was sometimes built around a cave or carved out by hand. The lower portion of a peasant home is most likely where the family lived. There was usually a raised platform at the back of the room that many archaeologists believe is the place where the family prepared and ate their meals, visited together, and then rolled out their mats to sleep. The upper portion of the house is often where the guest room — the kataluma — was located. In the case of a single-story home, the kataluma may have been as simple as a corner of the main living area that was set aside for guests. This model was based on a multiple story version of a first-century Hebrew home.

THE MANGER Mary laid the baby Jesus in a manger. Doesn't that automatically mean they were in a stable? Over the last several centuries that is the only explanation that seemed to make any sense, but first-century Bethlehem was not like the farm communities that have been developed since that time. When we read "manger," we tend to project our current understanding of where a manger should be located onto the biblical text.

Now many archaeologists believe that the lowest level of the common peasant home was where animals were brought in at night. This would have protected the animals from thieves and may have provided extra warmth to the family on cold desert nights. There was often a manger, a feeding trough for animals, which was carved into the floor or built into the wall of the main living area. This is not surprising because, even as recently as modern times, many Middle Eastern homes have lower levels with mangers built into them.

With this biblical, historical, and archaeological understanding in mind, let's re-evaluate the arrival of Mary and Joseph. Joseph and Mary were probably welcomed into the home of relatives. But due to the census, many people were returning to Bethlehem, including Joseph's other out-of-town relatives. Because the traditional guest room, the *kataluma*, was already taken, Mary laid the baby Jesus in a manger. Under the circumstances, a built-in stone manger would be unusual and humble, but a perfectly suitable place to serve as a temporary crib to lay the newborn Son of God.

WHAT ABOUT THE WISE MEN?

Let us reiterate this important topic. So where were the wise men the night of Christ's birth? And where did we get the idea that there were three of them? From a faraway land, the wise men followed an unusual star from the East, in search of the newborn king that they might worship him (Numbers 24:17). Naturally, they went to the palace of King Herod in Judea. Surely he would know the whereabouts of his successor. But the king knew nothing about the matter! Herod called together the chief priests and teachers of the law who told him of an ancient prophecy that revealed the birthplace of the child who would be king (Micah 5:2). So this scheming, paranoid ruler sent the wise men to Bethlehem, and urged them to return with news of the Christ child's specific location. The wise men did not return to Herod because they were warned in a dream that he was determined to kill the child king.

Then Herod, when he had secretly called the wise men, determined from them what time the star appeared. And he sent them to Bethlehem and said, "Go and search carefully for the young Child, and when you have found Him, bring back word to me, that I may come and worship Him also."

When they heard the king, they departed; and behold, the star which they had seen in the East went before them, till it came and stood over where the young Child was. . . . And when they had come into the house, they saw the young Child with Mary His mother, and fell down and worshiped Him. And when they had opened their treasures, they presented gifts to Him: *gold, frankincense, and myrrh.*

Then, being divinely warned in a dream that they should not return to Herod, they departed for their own country another way (Matthew 2:7–12).

So did the wise men find baby Jesus on the night of His birth? Or did they come later? Let's examine the biblical text.

In verse 9, the account of the wise men refers to Jesus as a paidion — a Greek word that can mean "young child." This may indicate that Jesus was no longer an infant when the wisemen visited — which could be why when the wise men did not return to Herod. He eventually ordered the killing of all male children ages two and under in Bethlehem and the surrounding regions — providing yet another clue to the timeline of the wise men's visit.

And why do we typically see depictions of three wise men? Well, the biblical text does not say how many there were, but tradition has numbered the wise men by their three gifts: gold, frankincense, and myrrh.

ALL TOGETHER As we consider all this information, we are compelled to paint a more complete and biblically accurate picture of the circumstances that surrounded the birth of Jesus. Joseph and Mary sought shelter, probably among relatives, but the guest room was full because of the census. So they may have slept in the lower level, which was perfectly natu-

ral in that culture. In fact, many homes had only one room where everyone slept. Luke 2:6 says that "days" passed by while "they were there" before the birth occurred. So, at some time during their stay (but not on the night of their arrival in Bethlehem), Jesus was born, probably in a humble peasant home, and laid in a manger that may have been located in the lower level of the house.

Now the picture is getting clear-er. But why did Jesus come? Why all of the fuss about the birth of this baby?

THE PROBLEM In order to re-ally understand the birth of Je-sus and the true meaning of it, we must first understand why Jesus came to earth. The birth of Jesus addressed humankind's greatest need — the need of a Savior. But that need didn't start in Bethlehem. It was es-tablished long ago, when Adam sinned in the Garden of Eden, when he rebelled against his Creator (Genesis 3:17). Because of Adam's sin, all of his descen-dants, including each of us, are born in rebellion and separat-ed from a Holy God (Romans 5:12). Humans have a universal problem. It's not lack of edu-cation or government. It is not overpopulation or even hunger. The universal problem that we all face and cannot solve on our own is sin.

All people are descendants of the first man, Adam, and rebel against the Creator God. This

rebellion is called sin. In the beginning, before sin, God gave Adam and Eve everything they needed in the Garden of Eden and it was very good (Genesis 1:31). He permitted them to eat from any tree in the garden except for one, the Tree of the Knowledge of Good and Evil (Genesis 2:17). He told Adam that if he ate from that tree, he would surely die (Genesis 2:17). The Bible says that Adam and

Eve rebelled against God's command and ate from that tree (Genesis 3:6). As a result, death entered into the world (Genesis 3:19 and 1 Corinthians 15:22). Because we are all descendants of Adam, we are, therefore, sinful from conception (Psalm 51:5). The Bible says that *all have sinned and fall short of the glory of God* (Romans 3:23).

In this sinful condition we cannot live with a holy God, but are condemned to separation from God. We are therefore subject to *everlasting destruction from the presence of the Lord and from the glory of His power* (2 Thessalonians 1:9). We live in a world that is filled with sin, death, disease, and suffering and everyone can see the problem, whether they believe the

Bible or not. One cannot live on this earth without witnessing and partaking in the suffering that human rebellion has brought to God's creation. But the Bible tells us God's solution!

GOD'S SOLUTION God was not surprised when Adam and Eve chose to disobey. God in His wisdom knew exactly what they (and we) would choose. Sadly, as a consequence of their sin, God had to kill animals to make clothing as a covering for Adam and Eve. This was the first sacrifice (Genesis 3:21). From that point on, throughout the rest of the Old Testament, God required animal sacrifices as a temporary sin covering — a picture of the perfect sacrifice that was yet to come to provide

the Lamb

The next day John saw Jesus coming toward him, and said, "Behold! The Lamb of God who takes away the sin of the world!
— *John 1:29*

the answer to the universal sin problem.

The Israelites sacrificed spotless lambs for generations as temporary payment for sin, but only a son of Adam, one who was perfect and without sin, could pay the price once and for all. In order to save us from sin and its penalty (death), Jesus Christ, the sinless, spotless Lamb of God became one of us on that special night in Bethlehem (John 1:29). He grew up and willingly died in our place on the Cross (Phillipians 2:8). And then three days later, He rose again, conquering sin's death penalty (Acts 10:40).

Jesus shattered the separation between God and us, and now offers the marvelous gift of eternal life to all who repent of their sins and believe in Him (John 3:16–18). He is *the Lamb slain from the foundation of the world* (Revelation 13:8).

THE SHEPHERDS When we understand the reason for the birth of Jesus, we can better appreciate the shepherds' role on the special night when Jesus was born.

Now there were in the same country shepherds living out in the fields, keeping watch over their flock by night. And behold, an angel of the Lord stood before them, and the glory of the Lord shone around them, and they were greatly afraid. Then the angel said to them, Do not be afraid, for behold, I bring you good tidings of great joy which will be to all people. For there is born to you this day in the city of David a Savior, who is Christ the Lord. And this will be the sign to you: You will find a Babe wrapped in swaddling cloths, lying in a manger. . . . And they came with haste and found Mary and Joseph, and the Babe lying in a manger (Luke 2:8–16).

We don't know for sure, but it is at least possible that the lowly shepherds, to whom the angels appeared that starry night, were guarding the sacrificial lambs. What we do know is that God chose these humble hired hands to be the first witnesses of the Good Shepherd, Jesus, the Lamb of God who would sacrifice His life to atone for the sins of all — a one-time perfect sacrifice, offered by the Father God Himself (1 John 2:2).

A NEW TRADITION The Christmas account is one of the most beautiful, powerful, and meaningful events in all of history because the birth of Jesus addresses man's greatest need — the need of a Savior. This Christmas, may we suggest that you start a new tradition: remove the nativity out from its hiding place under the tree and set it in a featured place in your home. Take the wise men and place them across the room. After all, they're probably still on their way! Then set aside a special time to gather together, open the Bible, and read the amazing historical record of Mary and Joseph, to whom God entrusted His precious Son.

ANSWERS TO THE QUIZ AT THE BEGINNING OF THIS CHAPTER:

Q1. Mary was in labor when they got into town, so Joseph had to take whatever lodging he could get. False — *so it was, that while they were there, the days were completed for her to be delivered* (Luke 2:6).

Q2. The Bible uses the Greek word kataluma — translated "inn." Kataluma means "small hotel." False — Kataluma is best translated "guest room."

Q3. The Bible says that Mary and Joseph spent the night in a stable. False — There is no mention of a stable, only a manger, but we now know through archaeology that there was a manger in the lower level of the average house of the area.

Q4. The innkeeper told Mary and Joseph there was no room for them in the inn. False — There is no mention of an innkeeper in the biblical account of Christ's birth.

Q5. The innkeeper's wife brought water and towels to Mary and assisted in Jesus's birth. False — There is no mention of an innkeeper's wife in the biblical account of Christ's birth.

Q6. The Bible says there were three wise men. False — The Bible tells us there were three gifts, but it does not tell us how many wise men were there.

Q7. The wise men were present the night of Christ's birth. Probably false — The text doesn't really say, but if you carefully read Matthew 1 and 2, you can see that Jesus could have been as much as two years old when the wise men visited Him. See chapter 6 for more details.

The

WAR

on

Happy Holidays!

Christmas

CHAPTER 20

Genesis
to Bethlehem: Why
Creation
is Important to
Christmas

During this season, there is particular emphasis on an event that occurred over 2,000 years ago in the town of Bethlehem. Christmas commemorates the birth of a baby prophesied about in the Old Testament. However, to fully understand the significance of the birth of Christ, we need to understand the history of the Old Testament that led up to this greatest of events.

Following the creation of the world, we read of the creation of the first man, called "Adam," from whom all of mankind is descended. When God created Adam, He didn't make him to be a puppet; Adam had the ability to choose and make decisions. God gave Adam an instruction to obey in Genesis 2.

Adam, however, chose to disobey God by eating the fruit of the one tree God had told him not to eat from. Because Adam was the first member of the human race, what Adam did affected all of humanity. The punishment for Adam's sin was death (bodily death and our immortal souls separated from God) — not only for Adam, but also for all his descendants.

In Genesis 3:15, God made a statement that actually sums up the message of the entire Bible and provided hope to Adam and Eve and their descendants (us!): there was a way to be saved from the effects of sin. This declaration summarizes the whole meaning of Christmas: *And I will put enmity between you and the woman, and between your seed and her Seed; He shall bruise your head, and you shall bruise His heel.*

The words "her seed" are actually a prophecy concerning the One who, conceived by God Himself, would be born of a

And the Word became flesh and dwelt among us, and we beheld His glory, the glory as of the only begotten of the Father, full of grace and truth.

— John 1:14

woman (actually a virgin): the baby who was born in Bethlehem — the last Adam. The first Adam gave life to all his descendants. The last Adam, Jesus Christ, the baby of Bethlehem, communicates "life" and "light" to all people, and gives eternal life to those who receive Him and believe on His name — to become the sons of God (John 1:1–14).

This is the message of the baby born in Bethlehem. It starts with the creation of a perfect world, and then, because of our sin in Adam, leads to our need of a Savior — which is why Jesus stepped into history 2,000 years ago.

Today, we talk about "keeping Christ in Christmas," but do we communicate clearly enough about why this is so important?

If we discount the story of creation, we remove the need for Christmas. And sadly, generations of young people are being educated in schools and by the media with evolutionary ideas about our origins. The erosion of Christianity in society is directly linked to the attack on the history of Genesis and the increasing indoctrination in a false history: that man is a result of millions of years of evolutionary processes.

The message of the two Adams is what life is all about. But if we want people to understand this message, we need to ensure that we show them that the history in Genesis is true, for otherwise they will not understand or listen to what is said about the Babe of Bethlehem.

CHAPTER 21

Winter Time

Worship: Santa Claus

or

Jesus?

As I drive through my neighborhood in December, I am confronted with giants dancing on my neighbors' lawns. A 6-foot-tall Scooby-Doo in a red knit cap sways in the breeze. An inflatable carousel that wouldn't fit in my living room spins a snowman, a reindeer, and an elf in an endless circuit. Santa can be seen in plastic light-up form, inflated fabric, plywood silhouette, and various other renditions — including catching a bass on a large fishing pole. Oh! Look! That yard has a manger scene surrounded by reindeer and candy canes and soldiers and snowmen and . . . you get the point.

If you brought someone from Russia to my neighborhood, what would they infer from the inflated and illuminated army? I sincerely doubt that it would convey the message of the Creator entering His creation to redeem it from the curse of sin. The manger scenes might raise a question, and the lit cross with the message "A Savior Is Born" would surely draw the visitor's attention (that's my yard). But these are certainly lost among the troop formations. So is this season about celebrating dancing snowmen and blinking lights or a Savior and the hope He brings?

Sadly, our culture has shifted its focus to the dazzling lights and away from a dazzling Savior. Commercialism has swallowed whatever Christmas used to be before it was this. Battles are fought over the very name of the holiday, and Santa Claus is embraced more freely than the infant Jesus.[1] Santa is an icon in modern culture, and his image is used to sell everything from soda to sports cars. How is a Christian to view Santa in light of the true meaning of Christmas?

SANTA'S ORIGINS As with many things in our culture, Santa has his beginnings in a Christian past. As the legends have it, the concept of Santa is rooted in the real Nicholas, Bishop of Myra, dating to the

fourth century. Nicholas inherited a large amount of money and used much of his fortune to help the poor. Nicholas gave freely to meet the needs of people around him, fulfilling the commands of Christ to aid the poor.

After his death, the Catholic Church recognized him as a saint — hence the common American usage of St. Nick as a substitute for Santa. The red clothing is likely founded in the red robes worn by bishops. The white beard and other trappings (e.g., reindeer, sleighs, elves, etc.) are likely adopted from various cultural influences being mingled together over the centuries. If you study the celebration of Santa (a.k.a. St. Nick, Kris Kringle, Father Christmas,

and Sinterklauss) around the world, the similarities are obvious, as shoes are substituted for stockings and the North Pole for the mountains of Lapland.

SANTA ABUSE The mythical Santa is clearly founded in a man who honored Christ with his life and his possessions. Nicholas gave freely of his riches to benefit those who were less fortunate than himself. This is clearly a fundamental Christian principle, as we see care for the poor proclaimed throughout Scripture (e.g., James 2:1–17).

Is that the same idea we see in the Santa celebrated today? The popular song extols children to stop shouting, pouting, and crying in order to earn Santa's favor and his gifts. This is clearly not the attitude that we see in the biblically motivated actions of the original St. Nick — and a far cry from a biblical attitude of raising children in the fear and admonition of the Lord.

I have personally overheard mothers using gifts from Santa to manipulate their children into behaving in a way that pleases the parent at the time. Such manipulation is entirely unbiblical. As Christians, we should discipline our children for sinful behavior because it is an offense against God, not because it is inconvenient or embarrassing for us. Using gifts from a mythical figure can only serve to promote a form of moralism that is alien to the gospel of Jesus Christ. If our actions are done to earn rewards for ourselves, are we not acting selfishly? This is not an attitude we should seek to instill in our children.

Our motivation for being obedient to God's commands should be out of an attitude of gratitude for the grace He has shown us. The gospel speaks of God's work in forgiving us of our sins — not because of the righteous acts which we have done, but because of what Christ did on the Cross for us (Titus 3:4–7). Nothing that we can do can make us righteous before God or make us deserving of His good gifts.

For by grace you have been saved through faith, and that not of yourselves; it is the gift of God, not of works, lest anyone should boast. For we are His workmanship, created in Christ Jesus for good works, which God prepared beforehand that we should walk in them (Ephesians 2:8–10).

Does the promotion of Santa lead to an exaltation of Christ? Since the two bring competing messages, I would suggest the answer is no. As Christ continues to be marginalized by society, our goal should be to magnify Him in our homes that our children would be impressed with His kindness to us shown on the Cross. This is the message the original St. Nicholas would have communicated.

MOMMY, IS THERE REALLY A SANTA?

A Christian parent must thoughtfully consider that Scripture is full of commands against deceiving others (e.g., Exodus 20:16; Psalm 101:7; Ephesians 4:25; 1 Peter 2:1–3). Persistently proclaiming the existence of a man in a sleigh with flying reindeer as fact can only lead to deceit. Please understand that I am not saying there is no place for imagination, but the level of emphasis on Santa appears to cross the line. The active teaching of Santa as a real person who performs real miracles to reward children for acting a certain way, in full knowledge that he is a myth, can only be described as deceit.

Any parent who teaches their children much of what is popular about Santa knows that they will eventually learn that it was all a lie. Lying is a sin and cannot be justified on biblical grounds. Have we bowed to cultural pressures to have our children conform to the ways of the world, or do we celebrate Santa so that Christ can be exalted? Rather than dealing with the root of sin against God, who is the definition of "good," the "goodness" promoted by Santa finds its roots in the humanistic philosophy of behavior modification.

As children grow, they will undoubtedly begin to hear others speaking of the mythical nature of Santa. They will ask and will expect an answer from the parents they have trusted. Since some may not wish to totally skirt the issue of Santa Claus (and it is difficult to do anyway), consider how it is possible to allow children to learn about the real St. Nicholas — and maybe even share in some of the fun of make-believe — while remaining honest with your children.

GLORY ROBBER?

If Santa has taken the glory from Christ in your family's celebration of Christmas, maybe it is time to seriously consider changing the emphasis. I understand that these are matters of conscience in many ways and that sincere followers of Christ will come to different conclusions. What

Santa Claus is a pagan corruption of a real person, St. Nicholas, who lived around A.D. 300

I would ask is that you examine your decisions in light of what Scripture teaches. If our conscience convicts us of sin in our hearts, we can bring that to God in repentance and know that He will freely forgive us because of what Christ has done.

This is the message which we have heard from Him and declare to you, that God is light and in Him is no darkness at all. If we say that we have fellowship with Him, and walk in darkness, we lie and do not practice the truth.

But if we walk in the light as He is in the light, we have fellowship with one another, and the blood of Jesus Christ His Son cleanses us from all sin.

If we say that we have no sin, we deceive ourselves, and the truth is not in us. If we confess our sins, He is faithful and just to forgive us our sins and to cleanse us from all unrighteousness. If we say that we have not sinned, we make Him a liar, and His word is not in us (1 John 1:5–10).

Rather than offering a plat-

form to chastise those with views contrary to this writing, I hope you will think and pray about how to bring Christ the worship He is due during this season when we recognize His incarnation. Let us all make the Word of God the authority in our decisions about celebrating this, and every, holiday — giving God the glory He alone deserves.

(Endnotes)

1   My purpose in this chapter is not to discuss the cultural shift to *holiday* and away from *Christmas.*

CHAPTER 22

From Creation to Bethlehem

In December, many Christians celebrate a holiday called Christmas. During this season, there is particular emphasis on an event that occurred around 2,000 years ago in the town of Bethlehem in Judea (today called Israel).

Christmas commemorates the birth of a baby — an event recorded in the Bible in such New Testament passages as Luke 2:1–20 and prophesied about in Old Testament passages such as Isaiah 7:14. The name given to this baby was Jesus. During Christmas time, many churches display nativity scenes. These exhibits show the newborn Jesus in a stable surrounded by various animals, shepherds, and Mary and Joseph. Such nativity scenes traditionally have also been displayed in public places (shopping centers, public schools, parks, etc.) in much of our Western world.

At Christmas, people sing special songs known as "carols." The words of many of these carols outline the events surrounding the birth of Jesus.

Because of the influence of Christianity and the birth of baby Jesus, history is divided into two basic divisions — A.D. (Anno Domini, Latin for "in the year of the Lord," Jesus) and B.C. ("before Christ"). As evidenced by the fact that Western calendars and historians count the number of years from this time, this was a very significant event even apart from religious aspects.

CHRISTMAS IS CHANGING

In much of the Western world today, nativity scenes are no longer displayed in public places. Such displays are now banned from many public parks and schools. Whereas Christmas carols used to be sung in public (i.e., government) schools, many times such songs have been replaced by ones that do not mention anything about Jesus and His birth.

Furthermore, more and more people are now calibrating their calendars with B.C.E. (Before

Nativity in the Wilkes–Barre, Pennsylvania public square.

Christmas in the Park

the Common Era) and C.E. (Common Era), rather than "before Christ" and "in the year of our Lord (Jesus)." The year-counts are the same, but the name of Christ has been re-moved.

In public schools in America, teachers and students are being urged or required by admin-istrators and lawyers fearful of lawsuits to use phrases like "Happy Holidays" instead of "Merry Christmas" or "Happy Christmas." Many advertising pieces during the Christmas season now delete the "Christ" part of the word Christmas.

Why was the birth of the baby Jesus considered so significant in the first place? And why is Christmas being viewed dif-

ferently today? What has happened to cause an event which has so influenced the modern world to be slowly erased from people's thinking?

THE HISTORY

To understand the significance of the birth of this baby, we need to understand the history that led up to this event. The only compilation of books in the world that gives a detailed history that enables us to fully comprehend the significance is the Bible. Over three thousand times the Bible claims to be the revealed Word of the God who created the universe and all life, and who has made Himself known to man. If this book really is God's Word, then it should explain the meaning of the universe and life — and it does. Not only that, but observational science continues to confirm the Bible's history as true.

Genesis (which basically means "origins"), the first book of the Bible, gives an account of the origin of life and the universe. It tells of the origin of matter, light, earth, sun, moon, stars, plants, animals, humans, marriage, clothing, death, languages, nations, and so on.

In Genesis 1:27 and 2:7, we read of the creation of the first man called "Adam." Interestingly, in 1 Corinthians 15:45, the one born in Bethlehem is called "the last Adam." To understand the reason for the "last Adam," you have to understand what happened to the "first Adam."

THE FIRST ADAM

The Bible records that on the sixth day of creation, God made the first man and woman:

So God created man in His own image; in the image of God He created him; male and female He created them (Genesis 1:27).

We read more of the details concerning the creation of the first man in Genesis 2:7: *And the Lord God formed man of the dust of the ground, and breathed into his nostrils the breath of life; and man became a living being.*

We are later told in Genesis 2:21–23 that God created the first woman from the first Adam's side. From elsewhere in the Bible, we learn that all humans who have ever lived descended from these two people

Eve

(Genesis 3:20; Acts 17:26, etc.). Therefore, all humans today are related because we have the same first ancestors.

GOD'S INSTRUCTION When God created Adam, He didn't make him to be a puppet; Adam had the ability to choose and make decisions. God gave Adam an instruction to obey in Genesis 2. *Then the Lord God took the man and put him in the garden of Eden to tend and keep it. And the Lord God commanded the man, saying, "Of every tree of the garden you may freely eat; but of the tree of the knowledge of good and evil you shall not eat, for in the day that you eat of it you shall surely die"* (Genesis 2:15–17).

ADAM'S FALL Adam, however, chose to disobey God by eating the fruit of the one tree God had told him not to eat from (Genesis 3:6). Because Adam was the first or "head" of the human race and all humans ultimately have come from this first man, what Adam did affected all of humanity. When Adam disobeyed his Creator's instruction (resulting in his "fall" from his state of perfection), that was the first sin. And just as God had warned, the punishment for Adam's sin was death — not only for Adam, but for all his descendants (including you and me) as well: *Wherefore, as by one man sin entered into the world, and death by sin; and so death passed upon all men, for that all have sinned* (Romans 5:12; KJV).

Why are we punished for what Adam did? As the head of the human race, Adam represented each of us, and because we all come from Adam, we have his nature, inherited from him. He sinned (disobeyed God), so we sin (disobey God). If it had been any of us faced with the decision to eat or not eat from the forbidden tree instead of Adam, the result would have been the same.

OH! THE NAKEDNESS After Adam and Eve sinned, Genesis 3:7 states that *they knew that they were naked; and they sewed fig leaves together and made themselves coverings.* In sewing fig coverings, it wasn't just that they recognized that they had no outer clothing — they also

133

saw that they were destitute of righteousness. Their innocence was lost. Adam and Eve were no longer perfect but were now polluted creatures in their hearts and their flesh. They were naked before the justice of God's law, and the fig leaves were attempts to cover what they had done.

However, no man or woman can hide their sinfulness from the sight of a holy God by their own doings. God sees us in all our nakedness and knows our impure, sinful, rebellious hearts.

The Bible says our attempts at covering ourselves (our "righteousness") are but *filthy rags* to the Creator (Isaiah 64:6). No ceremonies, rites, or attempts at keeping the law can change

this. Our works cannot take away our sin because our hearts are impure (Jeremiah 17:9). We cannot make ourselves acceptable before a holy, pure God because of the gross imperfection of our very nature — just as Adam and Eve's fig leaf coverings could not help them.

How can we ever be reconciled with a holy God? This is an important question since we are made in the image of God (Genesis 1:27), and as such, even though our bodies die because of sin, our soul (the "real us" that inhabits our bodies) lives forever. As sinners, we cannot live with a holy and righteous God, nor can we make it to heaven by our own works — we would be separated from God forever and live in

our evil, sinful states for eternity. What a horrible existence that would be. As the Apostle Paul says in Romans 7:24, *"O wretched man that I am! Who will deliver me from this body of death?"*

THE PROMISE OF THE "LAST ADAM"

In Genesis 3:15, God made a statement that actually sums up the message of the entire Bible and provided hope to Adam, Eve, and their descendants (us!) that there was a way to be saved from the effects of sin. This declaration summarizes what the Babe of Bethlehem is all about; in fact, it is the whole meaning of "Christmas": *And I will put enmity between you and the woman, and between your seed*

and her Seed; He shall bruise your head, And you shall bruise His heel.

What does this mean? Genesis 22:18 gives us further clues about the identity of the promised "seed" of the woman who will bruise the head of the serpent: *And in thy **seed** shall all the nations of the earth be blessed; because thou hast obeyed my voice* (KJV, emphasis added).

And Paul clarifies things in Galatians 3:16: *Now to Abraham and his **Seed** were the promises made. He does not say, "And to seeds," as of many, but as of one, "And to your Seed," who is Christ* (emphasis added).

Paul builds upon the use of the singular "seed" in Genesis 22:18. Here we see the extent of the infallibility of Scripture, down to the use of singular and plural words. The words "her seed" are actually a prophecy concerning the One who, conceived by God Himself, would be born of a woman (actually a "virgin"): the baby who was born in Bethlehem — the last Adam.

THE "HEAD" AND THE "HEEL" OF GENESIS 3:15

It is a great mystery to fallible, created human beings like us that the Creator God (Colossians 1:16) became flesh (John 1:14) so that as a perfect Man, He could become *sin for us* (2 Corinthians 5:21) by dying on a Cross to suffer the penalty for sin (the meaning of *"bruise his heel"*). But, because He is the infinite Creator, He has ultimate power, and thus He rose from the dead, overcoming the Curse. "Bruising the serpent's head" speaks of the mortal wound Satan received through Christ's victory over him at Calvary.

He is a defeated foe. His operation now is like the pockets of Japanese soldiers of World War II fighting after the surrender in August 1945 — they could still instill casualties and do much harm, but they could not win the war.

Jesus came to take away sin and conquer the power of the grave — death.

CLOTHED BY GOD God illustrated what needed to be done to Adam and Eve by a particular act. Genesis 3:21 states: *The Lord God made tunics of skin for*

135

Adam and his wife, and clothed them. God killed at least one animal — the first blood sacrifice — to provide the garments as a covering for their sins. It was a picture of what was to come in Jesus, who is the *Lamb of God who takes away the sin of the world* (John 1:29).

It is only the covering provided by God which can cover man's "filthy rags." The righteousness that enables a sinner to stand "just" in the sight of God is from God. No human being can put on the righteousness of Christ, for this can only be done by God (1 Corinthians 1:30). We can't rely on our good works (our "aprons of fig leaves") or on sacraments (e.g., communion, baptism) to stand just before God. It is only what

God does for us that enables us to be clean before our Creator.

HOW CAN WE BE CLOTHED?

Now if it is only God who is able to clothe us in righteousness, how can we obtain that clothing? The Bible makes it very clear in Romans 10:9: . . . *that if you confess with your mouth the Lord Jesus and believe in your heart that God has raised Him from the dead, you will be saved.*

When we acknowledge that we are sinners before God, repent of our sin and confess the Lord Jesus, acknowledging that He died and rose from the dead, we receive the free gift of salvation from our Creator and will spend eternity with Him.

THE TWO ADAMS The first Adam gave life to all his descendants. The last Adam, Jesus Christ, the Babe of Bethlehem, communicates "life" and "light" to all men, and gives eternal life to those who receive Him and believe on His name — giving them *power to become the sons of God* (John 1:1–14; KJV).

The first Adam experienced the judgment of God. He eventually died and his body turned to dust. Because of his sin, death came upon all men, *For all have sinned, and come short of the glory of God* (Romans 3:23).

The last Adam, Jesus Christ, also experienced the judgment of God — not for His own sins (He lived a perfect life), but for the sins of mankind. He died on the Cross to atone for sin (Isaiah

53:5; 1 Peter 3:18; Hebrews 2:9).

But He did not stay dead, nor did His body "see corruption" (Acts 2:27, 13:35–37). On the third day, He rose again, thereby overcoming the devil and the power of death for all people who believe in Him (Hebrews 2:14), and bringing resurrection from the dead (1 Corinthians 15:22–23).

This is the message of the Babe born in Bethlehem. It starts with the creation of a perfect world, and then, because of our sin in Adam, leads to our need of a Savior — which is why Jesus stepped into history to become flesh 2,000 years ago.

WHAT IS HAPPENING TO CHRISTMAS? Throughout the

world, generations of young people are being educated in schools, colleges, and by the media with evolutionary ideas about our origins. Sadly, they are being brainwashed into believing that the history in Genesis concerning the first Adam and the entrance of sin is not true. Logically then, they begin rejecting the truth of the last Adam, Jesus Christ.

If the history in Genesis concerning our origins is not true and therefore the birth of Jesus is insignificant, then why should nativity scenes be allowed in schools and public places? Why should students sing carols about a meaningless event?

The erosion of Christianity in society is directly linked to the

attack on the history of Genesis and the increasing indoctrination in a false history that has permeated the culture: that man is a result of millions of years of evolutionary processes.

Whatever the month of the year, the event that Christians celebrate in a very special way at Christmas is a message of hope for all people.

The message of the two Adams is what life is all about. If we want people to understand this message, we need to ensure that we show them clearly that the history in Genesis is true, for otherwise, they will not understand or listen to what is said about the Babe of Bethlehem.

CHAPTER 23

Getting Rid of Christ

Why in America is *Christ* being taken out of *Christmas*? If you told the average American 50 years ago that "in the 21st century, America will take Christ out of Christmas and make it nothing but a pagan holiday," I'm sure most would have responded with something like, "No — not here — that would never happen." But it is happening.

At Christmas time, I think it's important to ponder where America is as a culture and try to understand why this is happening. There are more Christian resources available in the U.S. today than at any time in its history—yet for all of that, America is becoming less and less Christian every day. The battle over "Christ" in Christmas is a sad example of this.

Abortion, gay marriage, the Ten Commandments being ripped out of public places, taking "Christ" out of Christmas — all of these issues are in reality symptoms of a much greater battle.

Think about it. Who is Christ? He is our Creator (Colossians 1:16). He is our Redeemer (Galatians 3:13). He is the Word! *In the beginning was the Word, and the Word was with God, and the Word was God. He was in the beginning with God. All things were made through Him, and without Him nothing was made*

that was made (John 1:1–3).

The real reason many in this culture want Christ out of Christmas is because they don't want to believe and obey the Word. This problem began in Genesis 3 when Adam and Eve rejected God's Word and wanted to decide truth for themselves. Ever since the Garden, this has been man's problem. Man wants to reject the Word.

That is why Answers in Genesis, with your support, must continue to stand up for the authority of God's Word. In this era of history, called a "scientific age," man has used supposed scientific evidence to discredit God's Word in people's eyes. As a result, generations have been led to believe that God's Word can't be trusted in Genesis. And

HAPPY
NEW YE

Season's
GREETINGS

Happy
Holidays

subsequent generations have applied this more consistently and now believe God's Word cannot be trusted from Genesis to Revelation.

We need to uphold the authority of the Word beginning in Genesis — countering the false arguments of the age that attempt to discredit the Word — and proclaiming the gospel that Christ is the Word, He is the Creator, and He died and rose according to the Scriptures (1 Corinthians 15:3). That is why God offers us the free gift of salvation.

Answers in Genesis and the Creation Museum are on the cutting edge of this battle over "Christ" in Christmas, because we're at the forefront of the battle in this age over the authority of the Word of God in the cul-

ture. And a battle it is!

Remember, if the history in Genesis concerning our origins is not true, the birth of Jesus becomes insignificant. You see, if there never was a first Adam, there's no need for a last Adam! The Christmas account, robbed of its context and historical foundation, becomes meaningless and easily forgotten.

That's why the final stop on the Creation Museum tour is the powerful Last Adam Theater. It follows the 7 C's of History (which are milestones throughout the Bible). When our museum guests reach this point, they have seen videos and exhibits bringing to life the miracle of **Creation** by God's own hand. They've seen the terrible consequences of the **Corruption,** as

the first Adam chose to disobey God.

Next, they witnessed the **Catastrophe**, in a room dedicated to a cut-away biblical representation of Noah's ark and dioramas outlining the disaster that shaped the earth as we have it today. In the second-to-last exhibit of the museum, they've learned about the **Confusion** God brought on by man's pride at the Tower of Babel.

Then, when they understand the context of sin and devastation brought on our world by our own disobedience, they're ready at last to hear the Christmas account in a way they've never experienced before — full of meaning and hope for everyone.

The gospel film in the Last

Confusion, Christ, Cross, Consummation.

Adam Theater is one of my very favorite parts of the Creation Museum. It's a moving dramatization of the life of **Christ** as seen through the eyes of people He touched, from Mary His mother to the soldiers at the **Cross.** There's a particular moment to enjoy when Mary places Christ's birth within the context of God's plan for all history: "One day, after I was engaged to Joseph, I was visited by an angel of God. He told me not to be afraid and that I was to give birth to a son and that I should call him Jesus. I asked how this could be since I was still a virgin. The angel told me the power of the Most High would overshadow me and that my son would be called the Son of God.

One day I learned that my son would be called something else as well . . . a lamb."

All "7 C's" work together, until that blessed day when we reach the seventh, the **Consummation,** when God restores life to the perfection He originally designed and those who are washed by Christ's blood can stand before Him forever.

It's no wonder most people think the Christmas account in the New Testament is no more than fiction, when the first four C's that give it meaning have been undermined and compromised by evolutionary/millions-of-years teaching! While the battle cries of God-haters get louder and louder, while lawsuits over nativity scenes proliferate, while more and

more of our society becomes entirely numb to the true meaning of Christ's birth . . . we must stand strong.

GOOD NEWS: THE GOSPEL OF JESUS CHRIST

Answers in Genesis seeks to give glory and honor to God as Creator, and to affirm the truth of the biblical record of the real origin and history of the world and mankind.

Part of this real history is the bad news that the rebellion of the first man, Adam, against God's command brought death, suffering, and separation from God into this world. We see the results all around us. All of Adam's descendants are sinful from conception (Psalm 51:5) and have themselves entered

into this rebellion (sin). They, therefore, cannot live with a holy God but are condemned to separation from God. The Bible says that *all have sinned and fall short of the glory of God* (Romans 3:23) and that all are therefore subject to *everlasting destruction from the presence of the Lord and from the glory of His power* (2 Thessalonians 1:9).

But the good news is that God has done something about it.

For God so loved the world that He gave His only begotten Son, that whoever believes in Him should not perish but have everlasting life (John 3:16).

Jesus Christ the Creator, though totally sinless, suffered on behalf of mankind the penalty of mankind's sin, which is death and separation from God. He did this to satisfy the righteous demands of the holiness and justice of God, His Father. Je-

sus was the perfect sacrifice; He died on a cross, but on the third day, He rose again, conquering death, so that all who truly believe in Him, repent of their sin, and trust in Him (rather than their own merit) are able to come back to God and live for eternity with their Creator.

Therefore: *He who believes on Him is not condemned; but he who does not believe is condemned already, because he has not believed in the name of the only begotten Son of God* (John 3:18).

What a wonderful Savior — and what a wonderful salvation in Christ our Creator!

If you want to know more of what the Bible says about how **you** can receive eternal life, please write or call the Answers in Genesis office nearest you or sit down with a Bible-believing pastor in your local area.

I pray for them. I do not pray for the world but for those whom You have given Me, for they are Yours. And all Mine are Yours, and Yours are Mine, and I am glorified in them. Now I am no longer in the world, but these are in the world, and I come to You. Holy Father, keep through Your name those whom You have given Me,[a] that they may be one as We are. While I was with them in the world,[b] I kept them in Your name. Those whom You gave Me I have kept;[c] and none of them is lost except the son of perdition, that the Scripture might be fulfilled. But now I come to You, and these things I speak in the world, that they may have My joy fulfilled in themselves. I have given them Your word; and the world has hated them because they are not of the world, just as I am not of the world. I do not pray that You should take them out of the world, but that You should keep them from the evil one.

John 17:9–15

CONCLUSION

In this book, we have seen how Christmas has come under attack, and we have been given answers to many of the challenges concerning this holiday. We know that Christmas was not born of a pagan holiday. In fact, that holiday, being a holy day, is still Christian, and the world must borrow that from a Christian worldview too!

We have seen that God's Word makes sense and that any misconceptions and alleged contradictions in Scripture are of people's own making, not that of the Bible. God is the ultimate authority in all things. We now have a greater understanding of the nativity, the Kataluma, the wise men, and many other aspects of Christmas.

I pray you understand that God is the authority and that when people go against God's Word, man's ideas are being elevated to a position as greater than God. I trust that you understand that this religion of humanism is a false one and that biblical Christianity is the truth.

Most of all, I pray that this book has been a blessing to help grow your faith. If you are have not repented and received Christ as Savior, I pray this book helps point you to Christ, the Lord of Christmas.

Merry Christmas